# How to Speak so People Will Buy

### Emily Schwartz

"I've been a business owner for more than 12 years and speaking with confidence is critical for success. Emily's tips on how to be a more proficient, interesting, and engaging speaker will completely transform your approach to speaking in front of any group."

- Dorothy Wolden
President, National Association of Women Business Owners,
Phoenix Chapter
Gravity Web + Design

This publication is designed to provide authoritative information in regard to the subject matter covered. It is sold with the understanding that the publisher and the author are not engaged in rendering professional advice or services. The information in this book is distributed without warranty, and the author and publisher disclaim any liability that is incurred directly or indirectly from the application of its contents.

All events recounted in this book, while based on true stories, have been significantly altered for both educational impact and to maintain the anonymity of those involved.

All rights reserved. No part of this book, including any worksheets or educational materials, may be reproduced, copied, stored in a retrieval system or database, distributed or transmitted in any way by any means without the expressed written consent of the author. For information on educational use, please contact the author at Emily@TheTimeDiet.org.

Any product names and services mentioned in this publication are the property of their respective trademark holders and are used solely in editorial fashion. Their use is not an intended violation of said trademark, nor does it imply an endorsement of any kind.

Copyright © 2014 Emily Schwartz

All rights reserved.

ISBN-13: 978-0-9850536-6-6

# DEDICATION

To the determined salespeople, the creative business owners, and any brave people who dare to have an idea they want to share with the world.

# CONTENTS

|    | Acknowledgments                   | i       |
|----|-----------------------------------|---------|
| 1  | Get Them To Listen                | Pg. 1   |
| 2  | Use "So What" Language            | Pg. 7   |
| 3  | Be Your Speaking Self             | Pg. 17  |
| 4  | Don't Fail at PowerPoint          | Pg. 27  |
| 5  | Tell Stories                      | Pg. 39  |
| 6  | Give a Sample                     | Pg. 51  |
| 7  | Quote Yourself                    | Pg. 63  |
| 8  | Be Funny                          | Pg. 75  |
| 9  | The Before And After              | Pg. 87  |
| 10 | The Subtle Sell                   | Pg. 99  |
| 11 | Handle the Unexpected With Grace  | Pg. 107 |
| 12 | Anatomy of a Presentation         | Pg. 117 |

# ACKNOWLEDGMENTS

A huge thanks to Dorothy Wolden, and all of my friends in the National Association of Women Business owners who inspired me to write this book so I can help countless more business owners for years to come. Thanks to my husband, Dan, who is a fantastic editor, sounding board, creative consultant, and cheerleader. People really *do* judge a book by its cover, so thank you to Gregg Clawson who worked tirelessly to create the look and feel of this publication. Finally, thanks to my daughter, Avery, who adds so much joy to my life every day and occasionally sat with me at my laptop for one of the many rounds of edits. Writing a book is a team effort, and I definitely have a winning team!

# 1

## GET THEM TO LISTEN

Alright, I have a confession to make. The title of this book is not entirely accurate. Yes, I will teach you how to speak so people will open their wallets for you, but that's not where we're going to start. Let me guess: you have an amazing business idea. You're an expert in your field, you've read all the success books, the marketing books, and the sales books. You have testimonials, a well-rehearsed and informative sales pitch, a package deal discount to offer, and a networking group who has agreed to listen. You walk in with confidence and a stack of business cards. You deliver what you think is the best presentation of your life…and nobody's interested. Within five minutes, the cell phones have come out under the table. The vacant stares and polite head nods have begun, and you begin to wonder where in the world you went wrong.

You are not alone. The problem is that you're trying to speak so people will buy, but before people will give you money you have to have something far more valuable and difficult to get…

...their attention. Before you get people to buy, you have to get people to listen.

**A Different Kind Of Currency**

In today's world, distractions are everywhere. We're bombarded with advertisements from the moment we wake up until the moment we go to sleep. We see ads in our emails, on our roads, on our phones, and in our cars. Instead of paying money to read the news, or watch a video, or stream a TV show, we watch an advertisement. We pay with a different kind of currency: our attention.

Because people's attention is in such demand, it is becoming more and more difficult to get. It's not enough to simply be better than the rest. You have to also be louder, or more clever, or more persistent. You have to know how to speak in a way that captures attention and keeps it. Then, and only then, can you sell to people.

So what grabs people's attention? A lot of different things, but just one strategy on its own is not going to do the trick. Speaking well requires a combination of factors that must work together in harmony.

**The Song That Won't Leave Your Head**

Think of it like your favorite song. What makes you turn up a song when you hear it on the radio? Sometimes it has lyrics you can relate to. Other times it has a good beat, or a catchy rhythm. Or it comes on at a time that directly reflects the mood you're feeling right now. More often than not, it has a combination of all of these things, and it's not by accident. Record producers and radio DJs know exactly what factors will cause a target audience to react well to a song and they select music accordingly.

Your speech is like the song on the radio you want your

audience to turn up. It needs to stand out among the constant static and noise as something worthy of their attention. I'm going to help you do that.

**10 Steps**

This book contains ten steps to help you speak so people will first listen, and then be so convinced of what they are hearing that they can't help but reach for their credit cards. The 11th step that I can't do for you is to practice. Speaking is a muscle that gets stronger with time. Once you master the strategies in this book, finding as many venues to use them will be the final secret to your success. Seek out networking groups, Rotary clubs, community organizations, and trade shows. Anywhere you can practice standing in front of people and delivering a fantastic presentation will make the next one even better.

Being a great speaker is more than just sounding good when words leave your mouth. It's about crafting a well-balanced speech, looking and acting confident, responding to your audience, and handling the unexpected. This book addresses all of those different qualities.

**Stage Fright**

For some of you, knowing which strategies to use when crafting and delivering your speech is only half the battle. The other half is making it all the way through without shaking or stumbling over your words. Fear of public speaking is extremely common and doesn't mean you're shy, awkward, or destined to be unsuccessful. It just means you haven't had enough of the right kind of practice. If you think about it, people who *aren't* at least a little terrified of public speaking at first are the crazy ones!

It's like being thrown into the deep end of a pool. If you are uncomfortable swimming, the thought of not being able to touch the bottom might terrify you. Being thrown into the pool the next day, and the next day, and the next day probably won't make you any better of a swimmer either, it will just make you more afraid of pools. You need a patient coach to teach you the right strokes so you'll feel confident in your ability to keep your head above water. Then you need practice applying those strokes and pretty soon you'll be swimming laps like a pro.

Consider this book your swimming coach. For speaking. Now jump on in, the water's fine.

# How to Speak so People Will Buy

Emily Schwartz

2

## USE "SO WHAT" LANGUAGE

Let me set this scene for you: You're hosting a game watching party at your house and guests will arrive in a few short hours. You're almost done preparing all the food when your spouse informs you that the downstairs toilet is broken. &^#($@. After a few minutes of cursing, you decide that with the wonders of modern technology you can fix this yourself and still make sure the party goes off without a hitch. You reach for your smartphone and type "How To Fix a Leaking Toilet" into the search bar of YouTube. You click on the first video and see this:

*(Long title slide with the name of the video. Slowly fades to black, then fades in to a friendly looking person dressed as a mechanic.) "Hi!" He says. "My name is Ben and today we're going to learn about how to fix a toilet. A broken toilet can be a real pain, but luckily, you don't need the expertise of a professional to make basic repairs yourself. I've been in the repair business for 20 years. I've repaired all sorts of home appliances. You might think you need to have a bunch of fancy tools to do a repair like this, but you'll soon find that it's very simple. I'm going to take you through several steps.*

*First we're going to figure out what the problem is with your toilet. There are many different things that can go wrong and diagnosing the problem accurately is important. Then, we're going to talk about how to fix the problem using minimal time, effort, and money, then we're going to..."*

Oh, I'm sorry, were you still watching? Probably not. You've probably moved on to a video that will actually show you how to fix a toilet instead of talking to death about it with a rambling introduction. You might have stumbled upon the single most informative and fantastic how-to video on the Internet, but you'll never know because it didn't keep your attention long enough to find out.

**The Attention Grabber**

When you speak, it's important to grab people's attention right away. The way to do that is *not* by starting off with a lengthy reading of your resume and qualifications or an outline of what you're going to talk about in the next twenty minutes. You need to start with something catchy. Something that precisely sums up the problem the audience has (or convinces them they *have* a problem they might not have thought about) and gets them thinking of a solution.

Think of the attention grabber of your speech as a billboard. When you're driving along the freeway, you only have a moment to read an advertiser's message. They have to make you look at it, get their main message across, and make it memorable, all in a split second. Think of some of the billboards you've seen. How do they accomplish those tasks? By being brief, clever, and un-ignorable. Apply those same tactics to your presentation.

**How To Write Your Attention Grabber**

Pretend you were not allowed to say anything in the

beginning of your speech and instead had to grab your audience's attention with a billboard featuring 10 words or less. What would the billboard look like? What would those 10 words be? Use that as a starting point for your attention grabber.

For example, one of the services I offer involves creating customized, professional-quality slide show presentations for clients who either lack the time, knowledge, or expertise to create one themselves. If I had to create a billboard that quickly conveys why someone should hire me, it would feature a picture of a person staring at a cluttered PowerPoint screen with tacky clipart everywhere. The person would be banging his head against the keyboard and appear ready to throw the whole computer out the window. The text underneath the graphic reads: *"I know what those buttons do. Let me help."*

That "billboard" is the starting point for my attention grabber. That initial idea might spring board into the following speech introduction:

*"How many of you have ever wanted to throw your computer out the window? OK good, I'm glad it's not just me. They're out to get us sometimes aren't they? Now, how many of you find that this tends to happen only when you're on a strict and stressful deadline? How do they know?? I get what it's like. I get what it's like to have a huge presentation next week and PowerPoint crashes. I know what it's like to feel like your graphics and text just aren't conveying the brilliance you wish to convey. You are a professional-quality expert and you deserve a professional-quality presentation. I'm going to help you craft that today."*

**Dissection:**

Let's dissect the attention grabber above.

### 1. It begins with a question

Questions are a great way to engage the audience right from the beginning. When you ask a question, people can't help but answer it in their heads. As people are answering your question to themselves, what are they doing? That's right. They are engaging in your presentation. Right from the beginning.

### 2. It focuses on the audience

People need to feel connected with what you're talking about or you'll lose them. Remember, people don't care about you yet. They don't really know you. They care about what you can teach them and how you can help them. The focus needs to be on your audience, not you. Reading your resume doesn't do that. Talking about a problem the audience has, does.

### 3. It's short

There is nothing worse than a long introduction. (Well, besides tacky clip art, but we'll get to that later in the book.) Make your introduction brief and to-the-point. Every word you say in the first 30 seconds should have a very specific purpose because in that time frame you're either gaining or losing your audience with every syllable you utter.

**So, How Do People Know Your Resume?**

So far, we've talked a lot about avoiding the lengthy resume brag in the beginning of your speech. The big question is: If not in the beginning, when? Remember, you and your company are amazing and have done a ton of incredible things the audience should know about. Here are a few ways to get that across:

## 1. Be introduced

Whenever possible, have somebody introduce you. It's more professional than introducing yourself, and instantly builds your credibility. However, don't leave your introduction to chance. Write one out. Remember, your introduction is still part of your speech and reflects on your presentation so you want it to be good. Write out a few sentences for your host to cover. (Notice I didn't say an entire novel.)

You should have one sentence about what you do, another sentence about who you've helped in the past, and another sentence about an award you've won or a book you've written. For example:

*It is now my pleasure to introduce Lauren Wilkinson. She is the owner and CEO of Webgraphics Unlimited. Over the course of 8 years, she has helped thousands of business owners increase their sales by 40% through website optimization. She was recently featured on Good Morning America for her book: "Unlocking The Secrets of SEO." Please welcome, Lauren Wilkinson.*

Short, sweet, and to-the-point, but again, an introduction like this won't happen by accident. Have this written out in advance and ask the host to look over it to see if he has any questions (i.e. get them to read through it once before they are standing in front of your audience so they don't stumble over your book title.)

## 2. Spread it out during the presentation

Once you're secured people's attention, then you can sprinkle in details about your credibility, but again, don't bombard people with your qualifications. Only list the things they are likely to care about. Emphasize results you've been able to bring to other people or qualities that will help people relate to you. For example, how have you been able to help past clients? What results have you generated for them? Put these in quantifiable terms whenever possible.

*"I've helped many clients increase their sales"* isn't as strong or memorable as *"This past year, I helped 100 clients double their sales in 6 months."*

Do you have a book out? Have you been on local TV recently? Or won an award? Say that! However, give the audience this information along with another piece of information to help them remember. For example, *"This year, I received the Chamber of Commerce Award for excellence in business"* isn't as strong or memorable as *"As I was graciously accepting the Chamber of Commerce Award for excellence in business this year, I was reminded of why I love my job so much: I love helping people."*

Resume bits are like the mayonnaise of a sandwich. Nobody likes a huge pile of mayonnaise thrown at them all at once, but it makes the bread, cheese, meat, and veggies much more delicious when presented as a package deal!

Just remember the cardinal rule of biographical information: say what's important to the *audience,* not what's important to *you.* Why should the audience care about your qualifications? Make sure you state explicitly how those qualifications benefit *them.*

### He/She Is Talking Directly To Me!

The goal of your talk should be to have all members of the audience feel that you are speaking directly to them and truly understand their wants and needs. When someone is having a one-on-one conversation with you, it's much more difficult to let your attention wander than if you're just one of a large group. That's why it's important to make each audience member feel like he or she is part of a one-on-one conversation. An obvious way to do that is by making eye contact with as many audience members as you can in a meaningful way, but another equally important way to make people feel connected is by speaking to their specific lives and situations.

One of the most blatantly simple pieces of marketing advice I've ever heard is: *"Find out what your target audience wants to hear...and then say that."* In this case, your target audience is the one sitting right in front of you. What are their struggles? What makes them laugh? What makes them upset? What brings them happiness? Those are the things you want to address in the presentation.

**So What?**

When writing each portion of your presentation, look at it from the audience's perspective. After you've described your product, business, or offering, ask yourself, "So what? Why should I care?" That's what the audience has in their heads the entire time you're speaking so it's better to ask yourself those questions in advance.

**Summary**

Speaking is the most personal form of marketing there is. It's fluid (you can adapt to your audience, unlike a brochure) you have a captive audience (unlike email) and you can instantly gauge people's reactions (unlike anything on a computer screen.) Use all of those factors to your advantage by using "So What" language to relate to your audience's wants and needs.

1. Have a strong attention grabber.

2. Don't bore the audience with a lengthy list of your qualifications all at once. When you do talk about yourself, make sure your audience knows why those qualifications

benefit them.

3. Make each member of the audience feel like the only one there.

Keeping your audience engaged is not easy, but giving them a reason to be engaged is the first step.

How to Speak so People Will Buy

Emily Schwartz

# 3

# BE YOUR SPEAKING SELF

"What are they thinking of me right now?" "Am I saying the right things?" "That guy in the front row hasn't looked up from his phone in 10 minutes." "I'm interesting, dammit, pay attention to me!"

These are all things that go through our heads when we speak in front of people. The action those thoughts translate to varies from person to person. Some people hear those thoughts and instantly convert them to fear or nervousness. Those emotions quickly become "stage fright" and can lead to a fear of public speaking. Some people hear those thoughts and convert them to confidence and poise.

I know what you're thinking. "How in the world can anyone take self-doubting thoughts and turn them into confidence?" Simple. Good speakers take self-doubting thoughts and use them to constantly gauge the audience and assess if the presentation is working. They are confident that they have many different tools at their disposal and if one doesn't seem to be working, they recognize it and try a different tool.

Here are two ways to turn negative thoughts into positive thoughts and actions:

*"That guy in the front row hasn't looking up from his phone in 10 minutes....what I'm saying isn't relating to him. I need to make sure I'm using examples that reach a wide variety of people in this audience."*

Or

*"That guy in the front row hasn't looking up from his phone in 10 minutes...oh well, his loss! Nearly everybody else in this room is hanging on every word I'm saying! I'm not going to change my winning strategy for one person!"*

Silencing your inner self-destructive monologue is essential to giving a winning presentation that sells.

**Your Speaking Self**

When people ask how to silence self-doubt and be a more confident speaker, one of the most common pieces of advice I hear is: "Just be yourself!" Wrong. Wrong, wrong, wrong.

I'm not saying you should try to be someone you're not, but if you're nervous or worried about saying the wrong thing, why in the world would you want to be yourself? Think about it. That "self" is anxious, shaking, and self-doubting. You don't want to be yourself. You want to be the speaking *version* of yourself.

Your "speaking self" is the same as your usual self in pretty much every way, except your speaking self oozes with confidence. Your speaking self is poised, articulate, and ready for action. When you speak in front of an audience – whether it's 10 people or 100 people – you are on stage and when you're on stage, you're acting. You might be a little nervous, but you're *acting* confident. You might be a little unsure of yourself, but you're acting like you know exactly what you're doing.

If the "speaking self" concept sounds a little too motivational-speaker-cheesy for you…well, get over it. Telling someone to simply "be confident" and "not be nervous" is as useful as telling something to stop thinking about a pink elephant. (You all see the pink elephant now, don't you?) Go ahead! Be nervous! Be unsure! Embrace it. But *act* confident anyway.

**Be Excited**

One of the easiest ways to act confident is to be excited about what you're talking about. After all, if you can't get excited about your topic, why in the world should your audience? I know that you're passionate about your business, (or, at the very least, passionate about the money a few sales could generate) but when you're nervous or start over-thinking the words you're saying, that excitement can quickly leave your voice. Don't let it!

Some people are naturally bubbly, passionate, and excited when they speak. They don't have to try as hard as those of us who don't wear our excitement on our sleeve quite as easily. If you're not an enthusiastic person by nature, never fear. There are ways to act excited that don't seem fake or over-the-top.

**Smile**

One of the quickest and easiest ways to show excitement is to smile. Haven't you noticed that when you smile, your voice changes? Try it. Read the paragraph above out loud with a straight face. Then read it again with a big grin. Do you hear the difference? The difference you're hearing is the addition of emotion. Your smile has helped add emotion and excitement into your words without even thinking about it.

People forget words, but they remember emotions.

An added benefit of your smile is that your whole posture changes. When you're smiling with your face, you end up smiling with your body too. You stand taller. You gesture more naturally. The whole package starts to come together. It's such a simple little fix, but I challenge you to watch for smiles now when you listen to networking presentations. You'll be shocked at how many people look genuinely unhappy when speaking in front of the group!

**Be Loud**

Another way to convey excitement is to speak loudly. If you're not used to doing this, it will feel weird at first. You'll think you have the volume turned up too loudly on the radio and you're shouting. That's OK. You're not. You're right where you need to be. When you speak to an audience, you can't speak at the same volume you use when you're having a conversation. Not only will people have difficulty hearing you, but it becomes very easy to tune you out. Remember, when you're having a conversation you only need to hold one person's attention. When you're speaking to a room full of people, you have to be the most interesting thing going on in order to hold their attention.

Being loud doesn't mean shouting or straining your voice. That will just make you hoarse and damage your vocal chords. Instead, you must project. An easy way to project is to speak with clear articulation. Sometimes we get lazy with our syllables, particularly at the end of words. This has a huge impact on how far your voice carries. Clearly enunciate each word with care.

Another way to project is to think of the sound as coming out of your face instead of your throat. Your face is where your voice resonates. Need proof? Hum the sound "mmmm" with your lips closed, as loud as you can. Do you feel the sound resonating around your nose? Isn't that cool? Now, hum that sound again, but once you get really loud, let your lips open as you change the syllabus to "meeee." Didn't that sound louder and fuller? That's how to think about projecting your voice.

Finally, you'll want to keep your throat loose and open. Go ahead and yawn. Did you feel how your throat seemed to get bigger? That's the sensation you should feel when projecting your voice. Singers think about these kinds of things all the time, and sometimes we think that speaking doesn't require the same kind of attention since we speak every day as part of our lives. Speaking for an audience is different. It's performing and we need to treat it with the same care as singing.

**...But Not Loud All The Time**

It's important to be loud, but it's just as important to not be *constantly* loud. When you never change your vocal tone, range, or dynamic, you run the risk of coming across as boring and monotone. Even if that monotone is loud, it still becomes easy to tune out if it remains unchanged for too long. That's why adding vocal variety is so important.

If you've been speaking loudly for a few minutes, try suddenly dropping your voice for dramatic emphasis. My favorite way to do this is to say, "Look, I'm going to tell you a secret..." then, say in a loud whisper whatever my very important point was. Any time you change what the audience is used to hearing, you grab their attention, whether going from soft to loud, loud to soft, or your normal voice to a different voice.

Adding pauses to your presentation can have the same effect as adding vocal variety. When you've been speaking consistently for a few sentences and you suddenly stop for a moment, the audience looks up. "Why did she stop?" I like to pause after reporting a statistic that I want people to remember in order to give it time to sink in. For example:

*"A recent study found that people fear public speaking more than death. (Pause). Think about that. (Pause). People fear public speaking….more than…death. (Pause). That means there is a significant portion of the population who fear this room of people more than a room full of wild hyenas that have the ability to rip a person's face off. (Pause). Wow!"*

Read the paragraph above out loud with no pauses. Then, read it again with the pauses as indicated. Do you notice a difference? Doesn't the second version sound more dramatic? Pauses also allow you to add repetition into your speech for emphasis without sounding like you're just…repeating yourself.

## Speak slowly

It might not seem like speaking slowly will help engage your audience. Won't it just put them to sleep? No. When we get even the slightest bit nervous, our natural reaction is to speak faster and faster. It's never in a purposeful way. Nervous or anxious rushing ends up sounding sloppy and unclear – two qualities which definitely *don't* engage an audience. While your normal self might want to speak a mile a minute, your speaking self needs to slow it down and speak purposefully.

It takes a great amount of skill to speak fast in a controlled way that keeps an audience listening. Don't attempt to speak fast until you can speak slowly. Chances are, you're not speaking as slowly as you think you are anyway.

## Stop Using Wishy-Washy Language

Finally, make sure your speaking self uses direct and clear language instead of wishy-washy statements. "Wishy Washy" language refers to mitigation statements. When we want to declare a fact, but want to distance ourselves from it and not take complete authority over what we said, we'll use mitigation statements such as, "I think that…" or "In my opinion…." Or "I'm not really used to speaking in front of a group like this, but I'm going to give it a shot."

Wishy-washy mitigation statements make you appear weak and unsure of yourself, and audiences don't give money to weak, unconfident people. Be bold! Take a stand! The audience *knows* you think and *knows* that what you're saying is your opinion. Own it! You're an expert on your topic, so act like it. You may feel the need to distance yourself from a declarative statement, but your speaking self does not.

## Pumping Up Your Speaking Self

By now, you're convinced that your speaking self needs to be the one presenting your material, but how do you summon up that part of you? Everyone has his or her own way to get pumped up before a speech. You have to find the way that works for you. Personally, I find that music helps. If I tell you my pre-presentation secret, you have to promise not to judge my behavior…Sigh. I can't believe I'm about to tell you this.

When I need to get pumped up for a presentation, I listen to "The Final Countdown" by Europe. More specifically, I watch the music video because if the driving, upbeat synthesizer doesn't inspire me, the 80s hair certainly will. Go ahead, Google it, and tell me it doesn't make you want to go do something amazing (or invest in a pair of a leather pants).

My point is, if there is a song that gets you amped and feeling confident, use it to help bring out your speaking self.

**Look Good**

Finally, when you know you look good you can't help but be more confident. This is not the time to be afraid of feeling vain or image-conscience. Looking our best helps us act our best and carry ourselves with confidence. Have a few go-to "speaking outfits" that make you look and feel amazing. Saving these outfits for speaking occasions also helps with the "speaking self" concept. It's like you're Clark Kent putting on your Superman cape to dive into action.

What makes a good speaking outfit?

### 1. Something that fits well

No matter what your size, a well-tailored outfit that fits looks better than hiding behind baggy clothes or ones that are too tight.

### 2. A step above the audience dress code

Always err on the side of too dressy rather than too casual. Arriving at a speech and being less formal than the audience makes you instantly feel insecure.

### 3. Compliments

Is there a color that you always receive compliments when you wear? Or, ladies, a piece of jewelry? Wear that.

### 4. Memorable

As a speaker, it's our ultimate goal to have people remember what we say, and then hopefully buy whatever it is we're offering. Let your outfit help you be memorable. Now, wearing a clown costume would certainly be memorable, but not in the way you're going for. You're looking for a bright color, unique accessory, or sharp combination that really stands out.

Looking good goes beyond your outfit of choice. Don't forget the power of a great haircut and manicure (yes gentlemen, you too.) Remember, when it comes to making friends, looks shouldn't matter. But you're not trying to make friends. You're looking to build business relationships and ultimately ask those people to give you money. Looks make a difference.

**Summary**

When speaking, the best advice is not to be your "self," but rather, to be your speaking self. There are several ways to bring out your speaking self.

1. Smile. Emotion is a great way to appear confident and relate to your audience and smiling is the easiest way to do that.

2. Project your voice. Speaking loudly and remembering to use vocal variety keep people interested in what you're saying.

3. Pump up your speaking self. Use music, a power suit, whatever will bring out your most confident version of yourself. Do it!

Confidence is an essential part of any good presentation and even if it doesn't come easily to you, with a little practice you can make it look easy.

Emily Schwartz

# 4

## DON'T FAIL AT POWERPOINT

Pretend that you're on a first date with someone. Everything is going well so far. You're at a fancy restaurant. You're laughing at each other's jokes. The chemistry is flying. You're starting to think this is someone you can really connect with. In an attempt to keep the conversation going, you ask about his college days, hoping you might find some shared experiences you can connect with.

Instead of answering your question, he pulls out a chart with sixteen bullet points and a cheesy, line-drawing clip art of a cap and gown. He then proceeds to read the sixteen bullet points to you, each one detailing a different fun memory he has from college.

Do you still feel that same awesome connection you felt before? I'm betting not. That's because *people* build connections, not text and graphics.

Now let's talk about that PowerPoint presentation you're using at your next speech…

## You Are Your Presentation, Not Your Computer

The biggest mistake people make when it comes to PowerPoint is thinking that the words on the slides are their presentation instead of the words coming out of their mouths. I'm not saying that you should never use a slide presentation while you speak. There are definitely right and wrong reasons to bring your computer with you to a speech. Allow me to share those with you.

## Right reasons to use PowerPoint

### 1. To emphasize key points

There are many ways to emphasize important points with your voice, such as speaking loudly, repetition, gestures, etc… Briefly repeating a key point on a slide is another tool you have at your disposal to add emphasis.

### 2. To add visual interest to what you're saying

Pictures, when used correctly, can add interest to your presentation, much like illustrations add interest to a recipe book, but don't take the place of the words.

### 3. To help clarify statistics or charts

Statistics add credibility to our presentations and can help educate an audience on why they *need* your services, but statistics are sometimes hard to conceptualize when you just hear them without also seeing them. Reinforcing them with your slides can help.

### 4. To add humor

Pictures can be funny, especially if they confirm a picture the audience already has in their minds

**Wrong reasons to use PowerPoint**

***1. To remember what to say next***

Your PowerPoint presentation should be for your audience, not to serve as your notes with bullet points to keep you on track with your presentation. We have a tool for that. They are called…notecards. And they should be used sparingly, not broadcast to the entire audience on a big screen.

***2. To serve as your hand out***

Many people print out their slides, staple them together, and pass them out as a hand out. When you know exactly what's coming next, do you pay attention? Right. Neither does your audience.

***3. To write every sentence you intend to say***

Every word you put on your slides will be read by the audience, and if they are reading then they aren't listening to you. You need to decide if you want your audience to read or if you want them to listen. (Hint: You want them to listen.)

**The Golden Rules of PowerPoint Slides**

To make an effective PowerPoint slide, you only need to remember three rules:

1. Less text is better than more text

2. Pictures are better than text

3. No pictures are better than low quality pictures

**These Slides Don't Make Sense!**

When looking at your PowerPoint presentation, ask yourself: *"Could someone understand most of my presentation by just looking at my slides?"* If the answer is "no," you might be on the right track to an effective presentation. If the answer is "yes," then why does anyone need you to show up to the speech? Just set up your computer and have an audience member advance to the next slide every 90 seconds.

Your PowerPoint should *support* the words you're saying, not take the place of them. The same goes for your handout. I love when organizations ask if they can get a copy of my handout for the people who were unable to attend the presentation. I say, "Well, I can forward you some of my blogs, or give you some of my marketing materials, or I'd be happy to meet with them one on one, but my handout won't make much sense without the context of my presentation."

*You* are the key in forming the relationship with your potential clients, so the focus of the presentation needs to be you and them, not your slides and handouts.

## So How Do I Make Good Slides?

Right now, you're thinking, "Ok! I get it! My PowerPoint is no substitute for a great presentation. It needs to support me, not replace me. So, how in the world do I do that??" I'm so glad you asked:

## Fewer Words, More Pictures

Never use words on a slide where a picture would suffice. Let's say you have a business that sells home security systems and you're speaking at a networking presentation. You might have a slide in your presentation with the following heading: (Please note that these statistics are completely made up, but yours shouldn't be!)

Reasons To Get A Security System

- A break in happens every 20 seconds in America
- It takes a thief 5.6 seconds to get in through your backdoor
- Homes with no security systems are three times more likely to be broken into than homes with a system
- Security systems give you piece of mind that you're doing everything you can to keep your family safe

That slide is very informative, but what do you notice? There is a lot of text. As you're speaking, the audience isn't listening or connecting with you because they are busy reading. Instead, I would make this four separate slides. Here is the first one:

20 Seconds

That's the only thing on the slide. It's printed in large type that takes up a good portion of the screen. The contrast is high. Perhaps it's red type on a white background, or white type on a black background. No fancy font, just clear, bold, and big. When this pops up, you say, "Guess what this number represents? Any guesses? It's the amount of time that occurs between break ins in America. That means that in the time since you saw that number, someone has been a victim of burglary."

Then, the next slide only says:

5.6 Seconds

And the next one:

3x

Finally, as you're finished going through the stats, you say "There are a lot of numbers and a lot of reasons why a security system is a good idea, but only one that really matters…"

That's when you click to your next slide. On this final slide is a picture of a Mom napping peacefully with her young daughter in her lap. The picture is high-resolution, and takes up the whole screen. Printed across the bottom are the words "Peace of mind."

**Dissection**

Let's look at the difference between the two presentation styles. The first one provides all of the information to the audience at one, the second one provides them only the numbers and allows you to make a connection while talking about them. The first one requires the audience to read, the second one requires the audience to listen.

Think about the last slide with the picture. You could talk for hours about how valuable peace of mind is, about how it reduces your stress, about how it makes you sleep better at night, etc… But none of those words you say will give your audience the same strong visceral reaction as that picture.

Everyone wants to *be* that picture: happy, peaceful, secure. It's something everyone can relate to, and it's something people are willing to pay for.

**How To Choose A Good Picture**

A good picture is one that grabs the audience's attention, takes up the whole screen, and is high-resolution so it doesn't look grainy. There are a few different ways to find pictures.

*Search Engines*

The easiest way to find pictures is to use a Google Image search. Actually, while I prefer Google for my other searchers, I find that Bing tends to do better on image searches for some reason. Set up the filter to only search for "Large" or "Wallpaper" pictures, as these will be big enough to fill the whole screen. HOWEVER, a huge word of caution about pictures you find on the internet. The vast majority of them are subject to copyright so you won't want to use them in a business presentation from which you hope to profit.

*Your Own Pictures*

If you have an inventory of digital pictures related to your line of business, you may be able to use some of those. Also, websites like Flickr allow people to post pictures and state whether or not it's OK to use them royalty-free.

*Stock Photo Sites*

My favorite way to get good pictures is through stock photo sites. Go look at a business blog online. ANY business blog, it doesn't matter. Do you see that picture of a team of three people in business suits smiling with their arms folded against a white background? That's a stock photo.

I like stock photos because it's easier to find exactly what I'm looking for. If I want a picture of a brown and white cow grazing in a field, with enough blank sky showing that I could type a sentence there, I can search for "brown and white cow, copy space" and have tons of options to look for. I can easily search for related images, images from the same photographer, etc...

While the pictures cost money, it's worth it to me because once I can have them, I can keep using my presentation and never worry about infringing on anyone's copyright. Some popular stock photo websites are:

iStockphoto.com

Shutterstock.com

123rf.com

Thinkstockphotos.com

All of them are good. I ended up using Think Stock because they happened to be running a coupon, and I've been very happy with them. Most sites will give you three options:

1. A yearly subscription with unlimited downloads,

2. An image pack for a limited amount of time, a limited amount of downloads, or both, and

3. Individual image downloads.

You're going to see the price of an individual download and freak out. That's because it's far more economical to get an image pack or subscription. Look at some of the prices, determine your presentation needs, and make the decision that works best for you.

## Using Funny or Metaphorical Pictures

When choosing a picture, you don't need to find something that literally depicts exactly what you're talking about. For example, if you're a business coach talking about ways to speed up your business growth, you might want to use a picture of a snail or a turtle to convey how slow the business growth will be without your services.

You can also use those metaphors to be funny. For example, perhaps you're a facilitator who helps people work through conflict management. You might say something like, "These strategies might help you at your next calm, peaceful, and respectful Thanksgiving Dinner with your extended family…" Then show a slide of a boxing match. This picture is funny because everyone knows Thanksgiving dinners can quickly turn into huge fights, even though we want them to be fun family gatherings.

## The Text

While you should minimize the text in a presentation, the text you *do* use needs to look professional. Resist the temptation to use ornate fonts that are difficult to read or a text color that blends right into your background. Choose one font and use it throughout so you have a consistent look from slide to slide. Make sure you're using a font that conveys the level of professionalism you're looking for. (If you're older than 16 and want to use Comic Sans, just stop yourself.)

Some of my favorite fonts are Arial, Palatino, Hoefler Text, and Gill Sans. Whatever you choose, make sure it is big, clear, and easy to read.

## How To Use The Presentation

The number one rule to remember when using a slide

presentation is to always use a clicker to advance the slides. A clicker enables you to keep talking while you click from one to the next without walking over to your computer and hitting a button, which can be extremely distracting to your audience. Also, sometimes your computer must sit in the back of the room because that's where the connector is. Without a clicker, you have to nod to someone else to change your slides when you're ready which is distracting.

When you click to the next slide, try to avoid turning around to look at it. Once we look at our slides, we tend to *keep* looking at them, as though we're giving the presentation to the slide and not the audience. If you need to give a quick glance over your shoulder to make sure the right slide is there, fine, but quickly get your attention back on your audience. Trust that your clicker is doing its job.

Finally, never EVER read from your slides. When you turn and read from your slide, nobody can hear what you're saying because you're not facing the audience. As soon as you take the attention off the audience, they take their attention off of you.

**Which Software To Use?**

"Wait, there are other choices besides PowerPoint?" Yes. While PowerPoint is by far the most commonly used presentation software, you also have other options. I dropped Microsoft's PowerPoint in favor of Apple's Keynote a few years ago. I think the animations and slide templates are easier to use in Keynote and find that the presentations look more professional. That being said, I sometimes have to convert my Keynotes into PowerPoints if I won't have access to a Mac at my presentation site, so you should use whatever you find easier.

Another option is the cloud-based "Prezi." If you've never seen a Prezi presentation, they are pretty neat. They abandon the standard "slide" model in favor of a zooming model that zooms in and out of different parts of your presentation. If you want to check it out, Prezi works on a "fremium" model, meaning the base version is free but if you want the presentation to be private or if you want to work on it offline, you have to pay.

**Summary**

Your PowerPoint is meant to support you, not replace you. Make sure to:

1. Use graphics. Graphics are memorable and add visual interest to the presentation

2. Use less text. When your audience is reading, they aren't listening.

3. Trust your clicker. Resist the temptation to look at your slides and read from them.

With a little practice, you'll be a PowerPoint pro in no time!

Emily Schwartz

# 5

## TELL STORIES

Once upon a time, there was a little boy named Trenton. Trenton wasn't very good in school, but he absolutely loved to play basketball. Every single day Trenton ran home from school so he could shoot a few hoops in his driveway before his mom made him come inside and do his homework. On every birthday and every holiday nobody had to ask Trenton what he wanted as a gift, because the answer was always the same: basketball memorabilia.

When Trenton had a big math test coming up, his mother was worried that he wouldn't make the time to study, so she made a deal with him. "Trenton," she said, "If you can get at least a B on this math test, I'll buy you the Kobe Bryant jersey you've got your eye on."

That's all Trenton needed to hear. You have never seen a boy study so hard. He stayed up late until he could barely keep his heavy eyelids open. He did practice problems until the lead in his pencil went dull. When he raced home from school with his B+ test clutched tightly in his hand, his mom was waiting with a present for him.

As he ripped it open, Trenton threw his arms around his mother and said, "Thanks mom! Thanks so much for this *new jersey*."

...."Trenton" is the capital of "New Jersey"

...and I bet you'll never forget that now.

**People Remember Stories**

Your audience will forget most of the information you tell them, but they will definitely remember the stories you share. If the first sentence of this chapter had been "the capital of New Jersey is Trenton" I bet you would have forgotten that information by now if it wasn't something you knew already. In fact, you might have skipped the sentence all together. But now that it's associated with a story you'll remember it.

Incorporating stories into your presentation is an essential way to keep your audience engaged. Not only are stories more interesting to listen to, but they are more memorable. Even if your story has little or nothing to do with your product or service, people will remember the story and remember you. Anything you can do to stay on your audience's mind after they leave your presentation will help you sell down the road.

Not only are stories memorable, but they help the audience relate to you. They help you see as a person, not just a salesperson. People do business with people, not companies, so building that personal relationship is key.

There are several different kinds of stories that are appropriate in different situations.

***Testimonials***

Instead of listing off the benefits of your product, service, or business, try conveying them in the form of a testimonial. When you put testimonials on your website, you're usually searching for that one sentence or two that perfectly sums up what results the clients achieved and why they would recommend you without question. When you're telling a *story* testimonial, you have the option to go further than that. You can now add context and details that help the audience picture *exactly* what kind of results they can expect from you.

If you're uncomfortable bragging, testimonials can help you get over that discomfort since you're not *directly* bragging about yourself. You're bragging about yourself through your client. A great story testimonial has three key components:

### 1. A detailed description of the problem your client faced

This is your chance to have your audience hear themselves in your story. Everyone should be thinking, "Yes! Me too! I have that problem!" It helps to choose a story with universal appeal.

### 2. A mention of how the client was hesitant to hire you at first

Not because of *you,* but because they weren't sure they needed your service. This is a key point. At this moment, your audience is having the same debate in their heads. *"Hm, this information seems really interesting, but I'm not quite sure I need what this person is selling."* Acknowledge that feeling by stating that your past client was having the same thoughts. Maybe he thought he could do this service on his own, or that it was too expensive, or not needed, but in the end, he was glad he made the decision to hire you instead!

### 3. Why the client ended up so happy, he couldn't imagine hiring anyone else, or purchasing any other product

What specific results did the client experience? How did those results help eliminate any initial doubt he may have experienced? Why did you enjoy working with this client? This is your chance to explain the specific result a client experienced and the specific results the audience could hope to experience.

It's important to note that testimonials aren't appropriate in all presentations. They work best at sales and networking presentations when the audience is there with the reasonable expectation they will be sold to. At a conference presentation, or informative workshop, where the sell needs to be much softer, testimonials can come off as too "sales-y" when the audience is not expecting that kind of tone.

### Fable Stories

A fable story is one that isn't directly related to your product, but instead conveys a message or moral that *supports* the mission of your product or service. I'll use the example of a popular, short story about the power of positive thinking. You've probably heard it before:

*An old Cherokee is teaching his grandson about life. "A fight is going on inside me," he said to the boy. "It is a terrible fight and it's between two wolves. One is evil-he is anger, envy, sorrow, regret, greed, arrogance, self-pity, guilt, resentment, inferiority, lies, false pride, superiority, and ego." He continued, "The other is good- he is joy, peace, love, hope, serenity, humility, kindness, and generosity. The same fight is going on inside of you – and inside every other person too."*

*The grandson thought about that for a minute and asked his grandfather, "Which wolf will win?" The old Cherokee replied, "The one you feed."*

You then follow up this story by adding a short message that you want the audience to remember.

*My challenge to you is that you feed the good wolf. Feed the good wolf. It's not always easy, but we must ask ourselves which part of ourselves we want to nurture.*

By adding that moral, "Feed the good wolf" you give the audience something short and catchy to remember that will remind them of your story.

I've heard Life Coaches tell this story at networking events because while it doesn't specifically speak to their business, the implied message is that the Life Coach can *help* you feed the good wolf in your life. What makes this story good?

### 1. It's short

Stories that ramble on for too long risk losing the audience.

### 2. It's universal

Most people can relate to the theme of this inner conflict.

### 3. It's metaphorical

The wolves are easy to remember.

### 4. It has a short take away message

By adding "feed the good wolf" you give the audience something short and catchy to remember.

(That being said, please don't use this story. It's over-done to the point that it has become cliché.)

## Personal Stories

Personal stories are my favorite because they help you

break down the wall between you and your audience. Personal stories are something taken from your childhood, family, or professional life. Like fable stories, they often contain a message or moral at the end, but instead of telling the story in the third person, you're telling it in the first person. What makes a good personal story?

## 1. *Universal appeal*

Again, stories with universal appeal are the most effective. The themes of struggle, overcoming fear, love, rejection, or family are ones which most people can relate to.

## 2. *Humor*

Personal stories are a great opportunity to inject humor into your presentation.

## 3. *Self-deprecating*

Showing the audience that you can laugh at yourself makes you likeable and easy to relate to.

One of my favorite personal stories to tell involves my first year of teaching. My first career was as a teacher and though I wanted to teach high school or college, my first job required me to teach kindergarten part of the week. I thought it would be a piece of cake, but quickly found myself drowning in a sea of angry five year olds. Despite these difficulties, I was too proud to admit that I couldn't handle this room full of tiny people and was reluctant to ask for help. It wasn't until I befriended a veteran kindergarten teacher and finally admitted that I had no idea what I was doing that my days started getting better.

This story is great because:

- Anything that involves children doing crazy things is funny

- It's self-deprecating

- The message supports my business. We can't be too proud to ask for help...and that includes admitting that you might need a little help with public speaking.

**How To Come Up With Stories**

Right now you might be thinking, "I would *love* to include stories in my presentations, but I don't have any." That just isn't true. You have plenty of story material whirling around in your brain, you just haven't organized it yet. Here are some strategies to come up with great stories:

### *Journal*

Before you go to bed at night, jot down some of the funny, interesting, or annoying things that happened to you. Did you have a fight with your spouse? Did you lock your keys in the car? Did you find a dollar on the street? All of these seemingly insignificant things can make great story material when put in the right context.

After you've journaled for a week or two, look back at some of your entries and ask yourself, "What could somebody learn from this experience? How could I make a moral out of what happened to me?"

### *Write Out Your Fears*

Many people share similar universal fears in life. What are you afraid of? What are your worries? In both your business and personal life? Chances are, other people share those worries too. What story could you tell that addresses those fears and worries? Remember, the best stories are those that have universal appeal.

### Try a New Hobby

A good way to have interesting stories is by being interesting. Haven't tried something new in a while? Make this the week you change that. Try a new hobby, go to a new place, meet a new person. Trying new things helps broaden your experiences to draw from.

I had never golfed before in my life. One day, on a whim, I told my husband I wanted to try it. We went to a driving range, got a bucket of balls... and I proceeded to make an absolute fool of myself. I couldn't hit the ball more than a few feet, I wore a low-cut shirt that flashed the world when I hunched over to set up my swing, and my hands ended up with blisters because I didn't realize those golfing gloves had a purpose. But you know what? I had a blast, and I now have a whole series of new stories to put into my presentations.

### Do the Stories Have to be True?

Yes. It's not OK to tell a story, *especially* a personal story that didn't really happen. Not only is it not honest, but you will get nervous when you're telling it. Part of what makes stories wonderful is that you don't have to think much about remembering what to say because you're just recounting events that happened to you. If you're making up the events, not only might you stumble over what you're saying, but you risk sounding disingenuous to your audience. Worse yet, if somebody manages to find out your story is completely made up, you look untrustworthy.

So, stories need to be true, but do they have to be *100%* true? No. Most of my stories are about 92% accurate. I often change names and small details to protect the identity of my characters, particularly in personal stories. Sometimes I'll combine two stories into one event in order to save time and make a shorter narrative. All events *happened*, but maybe not in the exact order or way I describe. Sometimes I'll paraphrase what someone said to make it more memorable or effective. There is nothing wrong with changing a few small details like that to make the story fit better in your allotted time.

**Be A Good Story Teller**

Once you have a great story, you need to be a great story teller. Even the best of stories can put an audience to sleep if they aren't told in an effective way. Be a great story teller by utilizing the following strategies:

*1. Use descriptive words*

Help the audience picture exactly what's happening to you by using descriptive words and phrases. Where is the story takings place? Describe the emotions at play.

*2. Show, don't tell*

Any time you can *show* the audience what happened instead of telling them, do it. For example, instead of saying, "Then I looked at my watch and I was shocked at what time it was," simply show them what happened. Look at your watch calmly, and then gasp in surprise. Show instead of tell.

*3. Build suspense*

Your story might be incredibly short, but you can build excitement by emphasizing the climax. What is the most exciting part of your story? Build the excitement in your voice as you approach that part.

*4. Use gestures and voices*

If your story involves more than one character, change your facial experience or voice when speaking as that character.

This doesn't need to be extremely dramatic, but it adds interest to the story and makes it clear which character is speaking.

## 5. *Be close to the audience*

When telling a story, if the room and set up permits, walk up closer to the audience so they are more engaged in the plot. You might even walk out a few rows into the seating to make for a more intimate setting.

## Summary

Using stories in your presentation is a great way to engage your audience and make your content more memorable.

1. Use testimonials, fable stories, and personal stories, depending on the situation.

2. Use journaling and new experiences to come up with new stories with universal or humorous themes.

3. Make sure your stories are true, but don't be afraid to change details where necessary to better fit the time allowed.

Always remember that the most important part of a story is the delivery, so build suspense and excitement as you speak. You'll keep your audience on the edge of their seats and repeating your stories years after they've heard them.

Emily Schwartz

# 6

## GIVE A SAMPLE

You're sitting at a networking event, your stack of business cards in front of you, and your "elevator pitch" all ready to go. As people start to arrive, you find yourself staring into space and letting your mind wander. "I'm so sick of these things," you muse. "I never get any business. I just end up feeling frustrated, like I'm spinning my wheels and not getting anywhere." You look down at the pile of business cards in front of you. "I suppose these old cards aren't helping," you continue. "Look how dated they are. That picture is ancient, and they feel so flimsy." You suddenly feel extremely self-conscience about not only your cards, but your ability to speak intelligently about your business in general.

You almost don't notice when the person next to you sits down and introduces himself. "Hi, I'm Keith," he says. "What do you do?"

You mumble through your elevator pitch as you try to think of how you're going to defend your business card as you hand it to him, since you're now convinced it's horrible. "Here is my card," you say as you hand it to him sheepishly. "Ignore that terrible picture. I'm replacing my cards soon. I hate these ones to be honest with you."

Keith smiles and takes one of your cards. "It's not a bad card!" he replies after a moment. "And that picture isn't as bad as you think it is. I think the reason you don't like your card is that there is nothing eye catching about it. There is so much information on here, that the eye doesn't really know where to look. I would take a few of these lines off and put them on the back to make it cleaner."

You stare at your card dumbfounded. "Yeah...I guess that would be a step in the right direction. Thanks!"

"Happy to help. Can I give you a call next week? I'm a graphic designer, and would be happy to see what other design tweaks I can help you with that will make your branding more effective."

And there it is. "The Ask." Keith just asked to contact you for a possible business relationship. He's going to call you, and probably offer to redesign your website, redo your business cards for you, and maybe even update your marketing materials. You're also probably going to meet at least three other graphic designers or web developers at this networking event in a few minutes...because let's be honest...everyone who has ever owned Photoshop thinks they are a graphic designer these days.

You'll probably get a follow up call from all of those designers you meet. If you were even remotely thinking of hiring someone to help with a redesign, whose call do you think you'd be most likely to return?

Probably Keith's, because you don't have to *wonder* if he does good work. He's already shown you that he can help you. He was friendly, he didn't criticize your (admittedly awful) business card, and gave you some free advice that let you know you could trust him.

**The Power of Samples**

Any time you give someone a little taste of what you can offer, you're giving them a sample. It doesn't matter if the sample is something tangible, or a piece of advice the audience can apply in their lives. If it's related to your business, and it benefits the audience in some way, it's a sample. Samples are a great way to hook an audience during a presentation because they:

***1. Make a presentation more memorable***

If you own a bakery, who is the audience going to remember? The bakery that let them try a cookie or the one that didn't?

***2. Build trust with the audience***

Giving the audience a little free advice or information that ends up serving them well shows that you know your stuff and you're capable of helping them further.

***3. Gives the audience a take away***

If the only thing an audience has to remember you by is your business card, you'll end up where most business cards do: in a pile or in the trash. If you provide them with information they can use, you'll stay top of mind every time that information is used.

**Why We Are Afraid of Samples**

Even though samples are a great way of increasing retention and engagement, many people are afraid to use samples in their presentations. It's an understandable fear. Here are some of the reasons people shy away from samples.

## 1. They cost money

If your business involves a product, rather than a service, your sample might be a tangible thing the audience can take away. Tangible things cost money and yes, that expense can really add up. Sometimes people are reluctant to give things away if they are worried about seeing a return on that investment. If you can't afford a sample for each audience member, try doing a raffle at the end. This also helps you gather more information on an entry form about each participant.

## 2. If I give them information, people won't need me!

Speakers in service or consulting-based industries might use *information* as a sample instead of a tangible product. Information samples could be something like, "5 Simple Tips to Improve Your Social Media Reach" or "3 Ways to Sell Your House Fast." While this information is definitely valuable to the audience, people are often afraid to give it away because they think clients will no longer need their services!

When you give away your information, it needs to be just enough to prove your usefulness and leave the audience begging for more. This isn't the time to give away your core message, or the key process or trade secret that makes your business unique. This information should be helpful, but secondary to the core strategy that really makes your business "tick." Besides, just because people have information, doesn't mean they have time to put it into practice themselves! For example, you could give me every tip and trick in the world about how to paint my house, and while I'll be more informed, I'm still going to call you to do it for me!

Furthermore, if a 30-minute information session renders your services completely unnecessary, then you might need to rethink how sustainable your business truly is.

## "Selling" the Sample

What you choose to give away is only 20% of what makes the sample effective. The other 80% is how you present it. One of the most effective samples I've seen was from a consultant who specialized in accounting, bookkeeping, and sales management services to small to medium sized business. After a fabulous presentation about managing sales leads, he provided every attendee with his template for tracking leads through the whole sales process: prospect to close.

The template was essentially an Excel spreadsheet with formulas that help estimate a prospect's likelihood of closing as they track through the sales process. There was nothing proprietary about the sheet and anyone with an above-average knowledge of Excel formulas could have created it rather easily. The great thing about the spreadsheet was the amazing way he sold it. He presented the sheet as an essential tool that turned the pile of cluttered business cards on your desk into an organized, streamlined process. He talked about the importance of systemizing complex processes so you aren't re-inventing the wheel with each lead. He built it up as a tool that would transform our sales process and generate more money for our businesses with less work, and we were all getting it....for free. He closed several coaching sales on the spot.

## Dissection

Why was his presentation of the spreadsheet so effective? Several reasons:

1. He identified the specific problem it solved. "How many of you have a stack of business cards on your desk of people you've met and have no idea where you met them?" He

emphasized how a cluttered sales process causes us stress, frustration, and leaves money on the table when leads fall through the cracks. He didn't assume we *knew* this was a problem. He directly pointed it out.

2. He was excited about it. This guy was definitely "geeking out" about how neat this tool was, and his excitement was contagious. If you're not proud of your advice or sample or information....don't bring it. The audience won't be excited about it either.

3. His sample gave a preview of the results people can expect from his coaching. I watched everyone's faces as he demonstrated this spreadsheet tool. He made leads tracking look so easy, so clean, so simple. Just listening to him talk made you *feel* more organized. Once people are hooked on that feeling, they are more likely to hire him as a consultant in the hopes that he can bring the calm and organization to other aspects of their business.

The most important piece of advice to remember when it comes to samples is that while you may *think* your product and/or information speaks for itself, it doesn't. You have to convince people it's useful. Use convincing words like "essential," "imperative," "crucial," or "vital."

**Saying A Lot Without Saying Anything**

There is a school of thought in the speaking/sales world that your presentation should give as little information as possible and instead sell attendees on a *feeling* that is only attainable with whatever you're selling. For example, you've probably seen this a lot with the "real estate guru" model. They manage to talk for an hour and a half about how to make money through real estate investing...and not tell you anything about how to make money in real estate investing.

Instead, they spend the whole time making you fall in love

with the freedom afforded by a lifestyle in which you don't have to work a 40-hour work-week at a desk job and instead rake in hundreds of thousands of dollars by "easily" flipping houses. They show pictures of past clients with huge checks, and smiling faces. In order to get the information to make this happen…you have to buy their course/DVD set/$997 conference registration…where you will receive a little information, and then another sales pitch.

Does this strategy work? Absolutely. Is it appropriate for all businesses, presentations and sales situations? No. In the wrong situation, this strategy comes off as sleazy, in-your-face, off-putting, and scam-like. (Actually, it can come across like that in the *right* situation too, but that's a rant for another book…) There is nothing wrong with selling an emotion. In fact, that's smart marketing. But if your presentation promises information and you deliver none, then your audience will leave feeling frustrated.

Instead of trying to copy the "guru model" as we'll call it, let's dissect some of the strategies they use that *can* work in a softer sell or more intimate speaking setting:

### 1. Excitement

If you've ever seen one of these gurus talk, you know they have energy to spare. That energy and excitement is contagious and demands attention. Energy doesn't have to mean running around the stage, shouting and gesturing like a motivational speaker on caffeine. Energy is moving with purpose, speaking with enthusiasm, and emoting with passion.

### 2. The Rush to Action

Halfway through a presentation, a guru will usually do something that makes the audience act quickly. *"This book is usually $49.99, but the first person to come up here and put a dollar in my hand can take it home." This carefully-planned strategy plants the seed in the audiences' heads that acting quickly brings great reward. "Oh man!" you're supposed to think as you watch someone race up there and get the deal, "If I had just acted faster, that could have been me." The guru is banking on you remembering this feeling when it comes time to sell his course/DVD set/$997 conference registration. "Buy *now* or regret later."

How can you encourage your audience to rush to action in a different setting? How about asking them to make a 24-hour action plan that they share with their neighbor about how they're going to jump start their journey to....better health, more sales, bigger business growth, a cleaner home, whatever it is you're selling. This encourages immediate action...that could also involve buying your product!

### 3. The Big Check/Big House Picture

Remember, gurus first sell an audience on a feeling, not a product. They do that by showing pictures of clients with big checks, huge houses, on expensive vacations, etc... What *feeling* does your product come with? Security? Piece of mind? Happiness? How can you tie in that feeling to the sample (be it tangible or information) that you're giving away?

### Selling An Emotion?

There is nothing wrong with trying to get your audience to feel a certain way. In fact, good speakers *want* their audience to connect with a certain emotion. Not only is it a great engagement tool, but people remember the emotions they feel even when they forget the words you said. You just have to be careful with what type of situation you're in and what the audience's expectations are. If you are giving a conference presentation where people are expecting to take away information, and you spend the whole time telling stories and showing pictures to spark an emotional response instead of giving any information away, people will be upset. We'll talk more about reading these situations in Chapter 10.

**The Costco Model**

I have one more thought on giving away products and information. When I think of "samples," I immediately think of Costco. I'm not going to pretend that this is a word association a majority of the population shares with me, but it speaks to my love affair with this warehouse store. I frequent Costco on most weekends. I try to time my trip to coincide with the lunch hour so I can feast on pieces of taquitos, chips and hummus, chicken salad on a cracker, or whatever other delicacies they've decided to put out as samples that day. (You're judging me right now, I can feel it.)

I used to think I was pulling one over on Costco. "Ha!" I'd tell myself. "I'm eating your chicken salad on a cracker and I have no intention of walking out of this store with chicken salad today." I have a feeling this is why many people are afraid to give away even the smallest sample at their presentations. "People will just take the free thing and not buy any more. Like Emily just admitted she does every Saturday at Costco"

Then I realized, Costco is having the last laugh here. Did I walk out of the store with chicken salad that day? No. But you know what I did leave with? $200 worth of other stuff, that I could have bought from other stores that *don't* enhance my shopping experience with six chocolate-covered blueberries in a plastic cup. And three months later, when I was desperate for a quick dinner, I *did* buy that chicken salad, because I remembered it was good.

Oh Costco, you know me so well.

**Summary**

The bottom line is that samples, be they tangible products, information, or examples of your expertise, can be effective elements to add to a presentation, as long as you:

1. "Sell" the sample. People need to be told why the information you're giving them is life-changing. Talk about your product with energy using high-value words like "essential," "vital," and "crucial."

2. Don't give away too much. Offer up helpful information, but don't give away the core of what makes your business tick.

3. Connect with the audiences' desired result. What result are you promising your clients with your service? Connect your sample with that result.

Samples are just another way of making your presentation more memorable, but like the other elements of your speech, it's all in how you present them.

How to Speak so People Will Buy

Emily Schwartz

# 7

## QUOTE YOURSELF

A few years ago, I found myself standing in the greeting card aisle of the grocery store. I needed to buy a retirement card for someone I didn't know very well, but respected immensely. First I looked through every card marked "retirement," but they were too flowery and wordy for my taste. Then I broadened my search to the cards marked as simply, "congratulations." Those cards were slightly better, but they seemed like something you'd give a teenager after they graduate from high school. I didn't want something with balloons and streamers on it that played a cheesy song when you opened it.

In desperation, I finally turned to the "blank card" section, which I quickly discovered should really be called the "I have no idea what to say to you, but here is a cute picture of a puppy" section. The frozen items in my cart were starting to thaw as my frustration started to build.

*"Why in the world are there no good cards here?"* I grumbled. All of the cards seemed to be for someone you've known and worked with for years, or for a boss you need to suck up to. Where were the cards that simply say,

*"Congratulations! I hope to one day accomplish half as much as you have in your career. Enjoy retirement. You've earned it."*

At that moment, I felt like an idiot. I knew exactly what I wanted my card to say. I was also a member of the "I own a computer and a printer and know how to use both" club. However, instead of making my own card, I had stood here for 15 minutes, in between the wine and the frozen food aisles, searching for the perfect piece of cardstock that I could purchase for $3.49, so I could have the validation of knowing an "expert" came up with the message.

So naturally, I bought the blank card with the puppy on it and called it a day.

**Relying on an Expert's Words**

When we're writing a presentation and we need some sort of snappy, inspirational phrase that supports our message, we often turn to experts. We scour quote dictionaries, inspirational websites, literature, and news stories for the perfect set of words uttered by a famous person that we can pull into our narrative. Why do we look to experts for these words?

### *1. Credibility*

When we quote a famous person to support our own message, it's like that famous person is endorsing our product. We believe that a famous person's words adds credibility to our message, and in turn, our product.

### *2. Memorability*

Famous quotes are usually famous for a reason. They are well-written, humorous, relatable, easy to remember, and inspirational.

### 3. *Easy*

Even though it may take a while to find that perfect quote to use in a presentation, it's often easier (and feels safer) to use someone else's words than your own.

**Use Your Own Words Instead**

There is nothing *wrong* with using someone else's words to support your message, but taking the time to craft your own pithy sayings can have some tremendous benefits to your presentation.

When you quote someone else:

- They are the expert
- People remember their words, not yours
- You risk adapting your message to fit the quote

When you quote yourself:

- You brand *yourself* as the expert
- People remember *your* words
- You can craft a quote that directly supports the specific message you wish to convey

**When Quotes are Appropriate**

Quotes make great transition and support material. When I speak about time management (while pitching my time management books and coaching services), I spend the beginning of the presentation talking about specific strategies people can use to tune out distractions, categorize their tasks, and organize their calendar. Then, at the end of the presentation I talk about the importance of avoiding stress and worry in the process. I need a transition between those two segments, or the presentation sounds disjointed.

To make that transition, I use a quote.

I say something like, "With all the things we have to do in our lives, it's important to remember that time management strategies are wonderful as long as we aren't too stressed to use them. After all, (here comes the quote) **Half the stress of getting it all done, comes from *worrying about getting it all done.*"** (Then I repeat the quote for emphasis.) "Isn't that the truth? Half the stress of getting it all done comes from worrying about getting it all done."

I didn't take that quote from anybody else. I needed something memorable so I wrote it myself. Then I repeat it several times during the presentation so people remember it, and have time to pick up their pens and write it down.

Quotes are also appropriate for:

- An introduction
- A conclusion
- Humor
- The moral of a story
- A tagline
- Your final slide

**What Makes A Good Quote?**

Not all inspirational or wise information make good quotes. Good quotes are...quotable. (That's right middle school English teacher! I'm defining a word with the word itself. What are you going to do about it?) When a phrase is quotable, it's short enough to be remembered. It stands alone without context or a setup. It might use repetition. It might contain a play on words or juxtaposed opposites. Let's examine two famous quotes by famous people, and my quote I shared with you just now.

*"Ask not what your country can do for you, ask what you can do for your country."*

  - John F. Kennedy

*"One small step for man, one giant leap for mankind."*

  - Neil Armstrong.

*"Half the stress of getting it all done, comes from worrying about getting it all done."*

  - Emily Schwartz

What do all of these quotes have in common? They all use repetition. They all stand alone without the speech, meaning you could see them on a refrigerator magnet, completely out of context, and they would still make sense. They are all short, easy to remember, and roll right off the tongue.

These three quotes also demonstrate my point about the benefits of quoting yourself along side "experts." I just put myself in a category with a President and the first man to walk on the moon. That's pretty lofty company, and whether your audience realizes it or not, they have now put you in the category of "experts I listen to" in their brain. That *definitely* increases your chances of making a sale.

### How To Come Up With A Quote

Having the courage to quote yourself is easy to find. Coming up with the quotes on the other hand, seems difficult, especially since you don't have the benefit of a PR staff or team of writers working for you! Luckily, coming up with quotes to use in your presentation is easier with these strategies:

## 1. Carry a notepad

It seems obvious, but the easiest way to come up with quotes is to write them down when you think of them. Strokes of genius occur at the most random, unplanned times so you need to be prepared to capture these ideas. Write down any word or phrase that pops into your head, even if it's not a perfectly formed quote. You can use these ideas for inspiration later.

## 2. Write frequently

Writing is a skill that gets better with practice. Try journaling, blogging, writing thank you notes, anything to flex your creative writing muscle on a regular basis. Even if the writing has nothing to do with your business, getting comfortable expressing your thoughts coherently translates into your presentation writing also.

## 3. Business brainstorming

Write down the top three results your business helps bring to people. For example, let's pretend you're a real estate agent. Your three results might be:

- *Finding your dream home*

- *Peace of mind navigating the home buying process stress-free*

- *Pride in welcoming people into your new, perfect home*

Next, jot down a few sentences elaborating on each of these three points. For example you might write:

- *Everyone wants to find the perfect home and it's difficult because sometimes it's more expensive than they can afford or the right feature combination isn't on the market right now.*

- *Buying a home is stressful when people don't know what to expect, especially if it's their first time. The unknown can be scary.*

- *People don't just want four walls. They want a home they are proud of and can see themselves inviting their friends to and spending time with their family.*

Next, look over your statements and choose the one that elicits the most positive emotional response. In my opinion, that would be statement 3 about pride. Now, elaborate more on that emotion. For example, you might write:

- *It doesn't matter how big or small the home is, when someone buys a house they are proud of they want to take care of it. It becomes part of their family. It's part of their identity. It's their castle and they are the kings and queens.*

Now look at all of statements you've written and circle words that stand out to you or connect with each other in some way. I would probably circle "perfect," "castle" and "pride." How can you put one or more of those words in a short statement that makes people feel the emotion you selected? (pride)

After a little thinking, I came up with this:

*You're not just buying a home, you're selecting your castle.*

Boom. Now you have a quote and I promise if you say it at least three times in the span of 2 minutes in your presentation people will write it down and remember you as the person who thinks they are a king or queen.

**The Bumper Sticker Effect**

Another way to come up with memorable quotes is to think of them as bumper stickers. Bumper stickers can only fit a few words or a short phrase and they are designed to be humorous or memorable. When you think of your quote, picture reading it on the back of somebody's car. Is it too long? Did it make you smile? Could you picture somebody shelling out $1.99 to buy your quote and stick it on their vehicle?

One of my colleagues in the speaking world, Doug Stevenson from Story Theater calls this a "Phrase that pays" because people remember it long enough to influence them to buy your product or service. As you're putting together your own quote arsenal, make sure your quotes are memorable and inspire some sort of emotion. Then use them frequently in your presentation, or consider printing some of them on your marketing materials.

**Using the Media**

Leaning how to be quotable is never more important than during a media appearance. Perhaps you've been lucky enough to secure a spot on local TV or radio in order to pitch your business or give an informational segment. These are golden marketing opportunities you need to maximize!

The most common mistake people make when going on these morning shows is thinking they are interviews. These are not interviews. A morning show appearance is two people taking turns talking. You need to have a set of 5 to 10 pre-formed sound bites that you'll integrate into your answers. A sound bite is a slightly longer version of a "bumper sticker quote" that will grab the audience's attention and give them something to remember about you.

Pretend a reporter is writing an article about your media appearance. What sentence would you want them to quote from you? That is your sound bite. Write them out and practice saying them over and over so the words roll right off your tongue naturally. If you stumble with "likes" and "ums," you disrupt your confidence and your message.

Talk with the producers or the host beforehand and ask what questions they will be asking and in what order. They are pretty good at guiding you through a list of 3-4 topics you agree on in advance. Nothing you're asked in the "interview" should be a surprise, and you'll need to know how long they need the segment to be so you don't ramble for too long.

**An Interview Example**

Let's go back to the example of the real estate agent. Pretend you've been asked to come on the show and talk about the three biggest mistakes people make when buying a home. You know the first topic is going to be about getting emotionally attached to a home too soon and overpaying. The host says this:

*"So Emily, you say that one of the biggest mistakes people make is overpaying. Tell me about that!"*

Here is an answer you might give to a friend over coffee:

*"Sure, so when people fall in love with a house, and decide that this is the perfect one, they really want it, they are willing to pay pretty much anything for it, even if it isn't really within their budget. They convince themselves that 'Well, just a few thousand dollars more isn't too bad' and pretty soon that becomes ten thousand, twenty thousand, and now you've bought a house you can't afford."*

There is nothing wrong with that answer...if you're speaking in casual conversation. On camera, that will sound rambling. There is no well-formed, concise idea for people to take away. Now, consider this answer optimized for good sound bites:

*"Purchasing a home is an emotional decision, but when you become emotionally attached to a particular home too soon, you risk paying more than what the home is really worth. Remember, the perfect home is one that has everything you want and is within your budget."*

That response is concise, easy to remember, and either of those sentences can be quoted as a sound bite. Being quotable means people are more likely to remember what you said, write it down, and call you.

**Summary**

Quoting yourself is a great way to brand yourself as an expert and have your audience remember *you* instead of somebody else.

1. Make sure your quote is short, repetitive, and/or humorous. These qualities make it memorable. If you can picture it on a bumper sticker, you're good to go!

2. Think of quotes by journaling or business brainstorming

3. The best kinds of quotes are those that evoke an emotional response. Keep that in mind as you're putting together your presentation.

With a few simple strategies, you'll be quoted like Eleanor Roosevelt or Yogi Berra in no time!

# How to Speak so People Will Buy

Emily Schwartz

8

## BE FUNNY

You're sitting in the lobby outside an HR manager's office. You've sent your resume out to dozens of jobs, but have only landed a handful of interviews, including this one. You're dressed in your best suit, you have all of your answers carefully practiced, and you're confident that *this* job will be "the one." You feel confident because these job qualifications line up with your resume perfectly. The job description was practically written just for you.

Another candidate sits awkwardly on the coach next to you waiting to go in. He's first. You try to glimpse a peak at his resume out of the corner of your eye without being obvious. *"My suit is better than his,"* you think to yourself. *"And this job is in the bag, there is no way he's better qualified than me…right?"*

You focus your eyes blankly on the wall across from you with a confident half-smile plastered on your face as he's called in. "Good luck!" you whisper as he strides into the office and disappears. Now you're faced with a dilemma: how in the world are you going to press your ear to that door and eavesdrop without getting caught?

You realize your best bet is to move to the couch closest to the door and be as quiet as possible. You can hear a few muffled sentences, but can't make out anything specific. After ten excruciatingly long minutes, you hear it: the last sound you want to hear from the interview right before you...

...laughter.

## Laughter Conveys Likeability

Why do you think you'd be upset to hear the previous job candidate laughing with the hiring manager? After all, it's not like you overheard his excellent qualifications, or anything about his resume. You'd be upset because laughter conveys likeability. When we're able to laugh with someone, it conveys comfort, it makes the person seem familiar, it's a way of breaking down a barrier between strangers that makes them friends. When we hear two people laugh, we assume three things:

1. They like each other

2. They are having a good time

3. They are happy

We want the members of our audience to experience those three things as well, so getting the audience to laugh while we speak is important.

Furthermore, if an audience will forget what we say, but remember how we made them feel, laughter is one of the easiest ways to produce a powerful and memorable emotional response. (Another strong emotional response comes from crying, however, I don't recommend that you try to make your audience cry!)

**Anyone Can Be Funny**

A common cynical complaint I hear in the world is, "Everybody thinks they're funny, but they're not." In the world of speaking, I find it to be quite the opposite. A lot of people think they *can't* be funny when they can. Anyone who has had at least one semi-amusing life experience and speaks with confidence can be funny.

Being funny when you speak doesn't mean brushing up on your best one-liners or knock-knock jokes. In fact, telling "jokes" like that can have the opposite effect. Instead of breaking down the familiarity barrier, you can distance yourself and come off as stiff and awkward. After all, who in the world goes around telling jokes like that in normal every day conversation?

Being funny when you speak is about injecting bits of humor into your speech through observations, stories, and self-deprecation. We'll look at each of those topics in detail:

**Observations**

We laugh at things in our lives every day. When you point this out to people, they realize they aren't the only people on earth who find it funny, and you get a laugh. The trick is to keep track of these observations as you see them. Start by asking yourself this question about your audience:

1. What sets of experiences are everyone in this room likely to have in common?

Do they all share a similar occupation? Are most old enough to either have kids or know a lot of friends with kids? Are they all from a similar geographic area? Do they all have common frustrations?

Figuring out what your audience has in common is a great way to start thinking of observations they will all relate to.

For example: I know that every teacher is annoyed that students seem to immediately lose papers as soon as they are passed out. When I speak to teachers, I reference this common experience they all share. I casually bring up that it's a scientific fact that any piece of paper touched by anyone under the age of 18 instantly disintegrates. It's a law of nature. This always gets a chuckle because everyone in the room can relate to the experience.

I also know that everybody who has ever worked from home knows how easy it is to be distracted by seemingly trivial things. This is why when I'm speaking to an audience in which most of the people are self-employed, I say, "Well, you certainly know when I've been procrastinating, because it's the only time every dish in my kitchen is cleaned." This is funny because many work-from-home people can relate to the desire to do housework in an effort to procrastinate.

Making jokes about something a group of people shares in common comes off sounding like an "inside joke." People love inside jokes because it makes them feel included and special. If you're having difficulty finding observations to share, you'll need to be more purposeful with collecting them.

### 1. Talk to people

Networking and talking to people of a wide variety of backgrounds and occupations is a great way to find commonalities.

### 2. Write it down

When you come across something funny, write it down. You may not know where it will fit in a presentation yet, but you'll find a place.

### 3. Listen

Don't speed through life with blinders on. Listen to the complaints and celebrations of people around you and look for commonalities.

### Stories

Stories are another easy way to add humor into a speech. If you struggle to effortlessly inject humor into every day information, telling a funny story might be a good place for you to start with humor. Some good topics for funny stories include childhood experiences, family, rookie mistakes, and "bad day" experiences. The next time something unbelievably frustrating happens to you, instead of feeling sorry for yourself, smile! You've just added another story to your story collection to pull out during presentations.

There are two quick ways to ruin a great funny story:

### 1. Tell everyone you're about to tell a hilarious story

Resist the urge to set up the story too much. First of all, if you say, "the most hilarious thing in the world happened to me the other day, let me tell you a funny story," now the audience is *expecting* to laugh. Humor works best when you've defied expectations, not conformed to them. Also, if your story doesn't leave them doubled over in laughter, you've then created an awkward situation.

### 2. Ramble for a long time before it's funny

The punch line shouldn't be the only funny part of a story. If it takes 10 minutes to get to the humorous part of your story, choose a different one. If the audience has chuckled a bit before you get to the punch line, it makes the conclusion that much funnier. Throw in funny details along the way and be careful to not let any one story go on too long. If it takes more than a few minutes to tell your story, it's probably too long.

**Self-Deprecating Humor**

Laughing at yourself is one of the easiest and most reliable forms of humor. It makes the audience feel comfortable with you, and they feel safe laughing because the person being joked about has given them permission to do so. Self-deprecating humor can come in the form of a story, an off-hand remark, or anything in between. Did you make a few silly mistakes at the beginning of your career? Tell us about them! Do you have a personal distinctive characteristic that people have teased you about? Tell us about it; it makes you memorable.

For example, I'm on the tall side of average. Kids used to call me "The Jolly Green Giant" growing up, which I was mildly OK with until I looked at a can of green beans and saw what my namesake actually looked like. I think part of the teasing came from the fact that I received none of the athletic abilities that tall people are "supposed" to have. In my workshops, I like to acknowledge this fact. At some point in the presentation, I'll say something like, "Before we go any further, I'd like to share two numbers with you, 6 and 2. Six is the number of feet tall that I am, and two is the number of years they made me play basketball growing up before they said, 'Please just let that poor girl join the band, it's less awkward and painful for everyone involved.'"

That little statement always gets a laugh (mostly because I think the audience is picturing me tripping on the basketball court) and it also makes them remember me as "that tall lady that came and talked to us."

**Universal Principles Of Humor**

Regardless of which way you've chosen to deliver your humor, there are a few universal funny principles that can increase your chances of getting a laugh:

### *Don't overstate it*

Jokes are the funniest when the audience is left to connect some of the dots on their own and not everything is spelled out for them. In other words, if you have to explain your joke too much, it's probably not too funny.

For example, this past winter I was asked to speak at a conference in Chicago. I began the presentation by saying, "First of all, I'd just like to say that I'm from Phoenix, and no, I would not like to check my coat…That's all I have to say about that."

I did *not* follow up that statement with an explanation. (Get it? Because it's hot in Phoenix, but it's really cold here. You guys are in the middle of a blizzard, and while you're used to it, I'm not, and am probably going to want to wear my coat indoors for a while.) No, this statement got a laugh because the audience was able to connect those dots on their own. (And also because geography and weather humor are always good for a cheap laugh and I have no shame.)

### *Defy Expectations*

When people see the punch line coming, it's never as funny. Surprise, on the other hand, is humorous. I saw a conductor at an orchestra concert do this very well. For an audience participation piece, he needed to split the audience in half. He turned around and said, "OK, this half over here, you're going to be Group 1. Now this group over here, I don't want you to feel like second place or anything, so you're going to be…Group B."

This statement is funny because he's defied expectations in two ways. First of all, nobody expected a joke in these simple directions, and secondly, everyone expected him to say "Group A." That would be the expected label for a corresponding group to Group 1 if he didn't want to say "Group 2." By saying "Group B," that group is still clearly labeled as the second tier despite the change in nomenclature.

## Give The Joke Time

A good punch line needs space, both before and after. This admittedly requires a high level of confidence from the speaker because even a split second of silence after a joke without a laugh can feel like an eternity.

For example, in some of my presentations, I tell a story about being stuck at a school when an armed robbery occurred across the street and nobody could leave the campus for hours. When a police officer finally escorted me back to my car, she said, "Now remember, if you hear gun shots, just drive faster because you'll be harder to hit." That statement usually gets a chuckle from the audience, but I get a bigger laugh by staying quiet for a moment. I stare blankly to my left, as though I'm looking at the police officer who is telling me this. After a few seconds of silence, I put my hand up to my ear and say, "I'm sorry, what?" as though I am in disbelief of what she's saying. That extra space after the punch line allows for it to be funnier.

## A Common Enemy

They say that few things unite friends like a common enemy, and "they" are right. Making fun of something that everyone in the audience dislikes is a sure-fire way to get a laugh. For example, when I speak to high school students about smart study habits, I like to say something like, "I know how stressful finals can be. Especially when that one teacher who thinks his class is somehow more important than everybody else's class, magically knows when all your tough tests are going to be, and schedules a huge assignment due on that same day." No matter how studious or lazy the kids, they *all* can relate to that situation and laugh at it.

To be very clear, the common enemy strategy must be used carefully. First of all the common enemy *cannot be in the room.* I would never use that joke when speaking to students at a school, only when they are at separate event I'm sponsoring. Also, if there is any doubt that the common enemy is not as "common" as you might think, don't use it. If a portion of the audience views that enemy as a friend, you're just alienated them for the rest of the presentation.

**Things To Avoid**

While we're on the subject of speaking carefully, there are a few things you should avoid when being funny:

### 1. Profanity

Using vulgar language is a cheap way to get a laugh, but don't be tempted to use it. Even if you're certain this audience curses like sailors, it's unprofessional and reflects poorly on your business.

### 2. Stereotypes

Making fun of any gender, race, or group of people is not OK in a business presentation, even if you *belong* to that group and think it's fine. I know stand up comics do it. They are paid to be "edgy." You're not.

### 3. Politics

Even if you're certain that you're speaking to a room full of the most conservative Republicans imaginable, an off-the-cuff jab at those "hippie liberals" is inappropriate. Adhere to the rules of an extended-family Thanksgiving Dinner: politics and religion are not discussed at the table.

**Cricket, Cricket**

The biggest reason people are afraid to be funny in a presentation is that they are afraid people won't laugh. A silent room of blank stares can be a terrifying thing and some people would rather just avoid it completely. It's true that being humorous requires a risk. At some point, you'll be in a situation where a joke will bomb. It happens to the best of us, the pros just know how to handle it.

Resist the urge to draw attention to your flopped funny. Just keep going and make a mental note to yourself that that type of joke doesn't work with that audience. If people aren't laughing, it might not be because you're not funny. Perhaps they are tired, or hungry, or cranky from other events that happened earlier in the day.

**Humor Promotes Engagement, Which Promotes Sales**

Remember, humor is ultimately just another engagement tool that you have in your toolbox. In a business presentation, we want people to response to the things we are saying by ultimately opening their wallets, but before we get to that point, they have to engage with us in other ways. Engagement can be demonstrated through listening, raising a hand, responding to a question, writing down a quote, or of course, by laughing.

**Summary**

Anyone can be funny if you just remember a few simple tips.

1. Stories are an easy way to start using humor if you're uncomfortable using it.

2. Timing is everything. Don't ramble on for too long, and give your punch line time before and after.

3. Avoid any topics that might be construed as offensive by some, even if you're sure some people will laugh.

With a little practice, you'll be leaving your audience in stitches.

Emily Schwartz

9

THE BEFORE AND AFTER

You're at a basketball game. There are still a few minutes to go before the game starts, and the stadium is just starting to fill up. As you settle into your seat with your large soda and oversized popcorn, you look up to see both teams run out onto the court to start their warm-ups.

One team runs briskly out onto the court and instantly looks ready for action. You aren't really paying attention, but you can see out of the corner of your eye that they immediately start setting up a passing drill. Then they move seamlessly into a free-throw practice, then a team huddle. It all seems very rehearsed, like they've done this before and they are there to win. Everyone looks confident, focused, and prepared.

Then the second team runs out from the locker room. One player moves immediately to the free-throw line and starts practicing his shots. Another dribbles the ball through his legs and practices turning from side to side, as though avoiding a defender. Two more players head straight for the water cooler and grab a drink. The coach pulls out his cell phone and fiddles with something while a few more players stand around the middle of court chatting. There doesn't appear to be any plan for how to use this warm up time and players seem to be doing whatever action strikes them in the moment.

If the second scenario sounds strange to you, it's because you'd never see it in pro sports. Professional athletes know that the game doesn't start at the whistle, the game starts as soon as you arrive at the stadium.

Even when the stadium is half-full, the scoreboard is still dark, and the warm-up music hasn't started, their actions still matter to the game. Their actions affect how the other team sees them, they affect how prepared they are to begin, they affect their focus, and ultimately, can affect the outcome of the game.

This is true for professional athletes just as it's true for professional speakers.

**The Presentation Starts When You Arrive**

When you arrive early, it's tempting to stand awkwardly off to the side, pacing back and forth as the audience trickles in. You might be studying your notes, fixing your hair, or fidgeting with your coat. All of these actions make you appear unconfident to your audience. They might not realize they feel that way about you yet, because they don't think they're paying attention, but they are. People give money to those who look confident and seem to know what they are doing. You want to *always* look like that person if you'll be asking your audience to open their wallets later!

Take care of tiny awkward tasks before you leave your car, or excuse yourself to the restroom. When you walk into the room you should pretend that you're walking onto a stage. No grooming, no pacing, no nervous fidgeting.

Another common mistake people make when arriving early is getting frustrated with their technology. Perhaps you're using a PowerPoint presentation as part of your talk, and your computer isn't working correctly, or you've encountered some sort of technical glitch. When we get nervous about technology, it's tempting to feel the need to make an excuse or acknowledge your lack of skill with phrases like, "Oh my goodness, does anyone know how to work this thing? I'm terrible with computers" or "I was having problems with this last week. I took it in and they said they fixed it. I can't believe it's not fixed yet. I can't believe this is happening."

Behaving this way only makes you seem flustered, incapable, and frustrated. If you encounter a technical glitch, calmly walk over to your host and ask if there is any way he or she can help. Don't panic or freak out. Just let them try to find someone to help you.

**What To Do Instead**

So if you're *not* supposed to fidget, pace, and freak out about technology, what in the world *should* you be doing during those awkward pre-presentation minutes?

*1. Smile*

No matter where you choose to plant yourself, smile as people walk in and actively try to look pleasant. I can't stress this enough. I have been accused of having "unhappy resting face" which means that my default facial expression looks like I'm not having a good time. I'm a bubbly and happy person, but if I'm not consciously trying to convey happiness in my face, I find that people think I'm irritated about something. Not a great first impression for an audience to see!

Maybe you're lucky enough to have "pleasant resting face,"

where your default look conveys a good mood. Congratulations. You don't have to try as hard.

## 2. Greet People

Even if you're speaking to a group you're unfamiliar with, or not a member of, greet people as they come in the door. Give a pleasant hello and either a handshake or a wave. When you say hello with a smile, people can't help but smile back. Don't you want your audience to be in a good mood when you speak to them?

Once you've said hello, you can walk around the room and pick a few people to learn a little bit more about.

## 3. Talk To People

This is the most important point of all. Its essential to talk to a few members of your audience before you begin. This gives you a feel for who your audience is, what their backgrounds are, and what kinds of concerns they have. Talking to people also creates a deeper relationship that you can reference during the presentation.

For example, if I find out someone is from Southern California, like I am, I'll try to reference that in the presentation. Or, if I find out someone has an interesting hobby, just got married, moved recently, or just had a baby, I'll find a way to bring that up too. If people have already had a brief conversation with you, then you're speaking to them as a friend, not a stranger, and people are far more likely to listen to (and give money to) friends.

## My Interesting Experience

One time, a meeting organizer called me at the last minute to fill an opening in their conference schedule. I was happy to step in and help and speak about time management. This would also be a great opportunity to pitch my book:

*The Time Diet: Digestible Time Management* that I sell during conferences.

I asked him my standard questions about who the audience would be, what experiences they had, and what problems they were seeking to solve. He told me that I'd be speaking to salespeople who sold vaccines and medicine to veterinarians. "Perfect!" I thought. "I love animals, this will be an easy audience to relate to."

When I arrived at the event, most of the audience was in another session. Rather than seeking out one of the people at the registration table to talk to, I sat awkwardly in the hall waiting for my turn. Against my better judgment, I didn't seek out the few people passing by to say hello or introduce myself.

When I walked into the room to begin, I had about 3 minutes to get set up and begin speaking. I was so focused on getting my technology together, that I didn't take time to notice anyone in the audience. I touched base with my host for about 30 seconds before beginning my talk.

"Alright!" I said, "So these people all work with veterinarians right? I'm excited to meet everyone, I'm such a dog person."

He looked at me blankly and said, "Oh, I guess I should have been more clear. They all work in the dairy industry. Most people here work on dairy farms."

I froze. What? I had prepared jokes and stories about dogs and cats. Other animals go to veterinarians? Silly question. Of course they do. I looked up at the audience and saw a packed room of people in jeans, flannel shirts, and trucker hats. I suddenly felt extremely awkward in my tailored grey suit. I realized that when my host had told me there would be people here from all over the western region, he didn't exactly mean the Las Vegas Strip and Downtown Los

Angeles.

I walked up on stage and starting talking, but all my jokes were falling flat. All of my examples I had prepared seemed suddenly irrelevant as I tried to wrack my brain for anything, *anything* that I knew about dairy farming. I struggled to get even the most subtle audience reaction, and while the meeting host told me he loved the presentation, I didn't end up selling any books afterwards. I had *not* connected with that audience.

On the drive home, I started to think of a million different things I could have said. My grandmother grew up on a farm and I always wanted to see it. I have immense respect for farmers because I think they work harder than most professions put together. In elementary school, I took third place in a milk-drinking contest at the county fair (and still have the ribbon to prove it.) All of these ways to build connections with the audience seemed so obvious now, but I was caught off guard because I hadn't prepared well enough nor had I talked to audience members beforehand.

Speaking with audience members helps to eliminate surprises when you speak, makes the audience more comfortable with you, helps you build up a connection before your presentation even starts, and helps lay the ground work for a possible sale later on.

**During The Talk**

The time for personal interaction doesn't end once the presentation begins. You can keep up that personal connection while you speak in two ways:

***1. Eye Contact***

Making sustained eye contact with people in various parts of the room while you speak helps keep everyone engaged.

Remember, you want all audience members to think you are speaking specifically to *them*, not necessarily the person next to them. Eye contact is a great way of saying, "Yes, you! I'm talking to you. You matter!"

## 2. *Moving Around*

If the room setup permits, try to walk around the room while you speak. This serves two purposes. First of all, it adds visual interest. When you're standing in one place, it's easy for the audience to zone out as they stare at one spot in the room for an extended period of time. If you're moving around, they need to shift their focus and attention, which keeps them interested and attentive. Secondly, moving around means you'll be in closer proximity to a wider selection of your audience, and the closer you are, the more people will pay attention.

When you're behind a lectern, you seem far away to the audience, because you have a barrier between you and them. Moving around helps remove that barrier. Teachers do this with their students. It's called "Management by Wandering Around" and it's extremely effective at keeping people's attention. Just make your pacing slow and purposefully. Walking back and forth too quickly or constantly can seem fidgety and distracting.

**After the Talk**

Just like the speech *starts* when you walk into the room, the speech doesn't *stop* until you're back in your car. The way you end a presentation, and your actions immediately afterwards, can have a huge impact on your future sales.

*"Well, that pretty much covers it! Thank you all for having me. Let's see, how are we doing on time? I guess we have time for a few questions. Does anybody have any questions?"*

The paragraph above is how far too many people end their presentations. Think if a fireworks display ended that way. Instead of the big finish in which all the rockets go off at once, the sky is ablaze with lights and everyone cheers, the show just fizzled out with one last burst of light and then the sky went quiet. How would you feel after an ending like that? I'm guessing that even if the rest of the fireworks show was amazing, without the big finish, you'd leave saying, "Well, that was OK."

Don't just let your presentation fizzle out and stop. End it on a high note with a good story, a key message, or a strong take-away. For example:

*"Finally ladies and gentlemen, good graphic design isn't about painting pretty pictures, it's about capturing the essence of not only your brand but also yourself. It's my hope that as you get on with your day today, you'll go do something worth capturing. Thank you."*

Ending on a strong note like this lets everyone know it's time to clap. When people give you a loud round of applause at the end of a presentation, the audience is more likely to remember your speech as being "good" than if it ends in silence. A clear, strong ending also leaves people feeling inspired and happy (and happy people buy things).

**What About Questions?**

We're conditioned to end our presentations with, "Does anybody have any questions?" You can still make time for questions after the presentation ends. After everyone claps, and before you turn the time back over to your host, say something simple and direct like, "Before we wrap up, does anyone have any questions I can address?"

However, consider if you even want to open the floor up for questions at all. Questions can eat up a lot of time if you have an audience member who enjoys listening to himself talk. Also, if you get off-topic requests or a question you don't know, you might end up at a loss for words. I like to tell people that I'd love to answer their questions individually and hope they will come up and talk to me afterwards. This allows me to form a closer relationship with audience members afterwards, I can go into more detail with questions that wouldn't necessarily pertain to the whole group, and I find more people are likely to buy my books when I have a "crowd" around me afterwards than when I'm just closing up my computer by myself.

If you do decide to answer questions, remember these three tips:

### 1. Keep it Limited

Just because 20 people raised their hands, that doesn't mean you have to answer 20 questions. Limit your questions to 2 or 3.

### 2. Keep it On Topic

If someone asks an extremely specific or irrelevant question, smile and say you want to give that answer a little more time and could they meet with you afterwards.

### 3. Keep it Positive

Sometimes people ask "questions" that aren't really questions at all. It's just an opportunity for them to say publicly that they feel you're wrong about something and they're right. Don't cater to that behavior. Keep a smile on your face and invite them to come up and speak with you afterwards.

### What About "The Sell?"

If a "hard sell" is appropriate in your speaking situation,

you can definitely include that at the end, but not as the closing to your speech. Remember, nobody claps after a sales pitch and you want your presentation to end strongly, rather than just sort of stop. Either include your sell before the ending your presentation, or end the presentation, and then give the sell. You'll decide which is best based on the situation.

**Linger Around**

I've never understood why speakers bolt for the door as soon as they are finished speaking, or immediately start fiddling with their computer, unplugging their technology, and putting away their hand outs. The best thing you can do to form potential client relationships is to stick around until everyone else leaves. Make yourself available to answer questions. Move toward the middle or back of the room so people need to pass you in order to leave. If you're busy putting all of your things away, people might be wary to approach you. Look as approachable as possible by leaving all the packing up for later.

Sometimes you'll find that one person will come up to you afterwards and want to monopolize your time. This means that others will miss out on a chance to talk to you. If you sense that other people are waiting and someone is taking up all of your time, it's not rude to ask if you can pause the conversation while you answer a few other questions. Try something like, "I'm going to pause you right there because I have a lot to say about that and I want to give you a thorough answer. Can I take a few of these questions and then we can continue?"

**Product Placement**

Finally, if you sell a product, rather than a service, chances are you brought some of that product with you to sell after the presentation. Where you place this product in the room matters. People like to touch an object before they buy it, so put them in a place toward the back of the room where people can peruse on their way out. Not only will people be forced to pass by your wares as they leave, but people are far more likely to stop and look if they don't feel as though they'll be pressured to buy. If your merchandise table is at the front of the room and you're standing right next to it, people may feel intimidated about coming up there to look and may just leave instead, even if they initially had an interest in your product. Give people space to browse without feeling suffocated.

**Summary**

Your presentation lasts for the entire time you're in the room, not just during the 30 minutes you're actually speaking.

1. Talk to audience members beforehand to get a feel for their experience and needs.

2. Make eye contact and move around the room during the presentation to make everyone feel included.

3. End the presentation conclusively and let people clap. Take questions either before or after the ending.

The audience may not realize how much they pay attention to your actions before and after your presentation, but they definitely do.

Emily Schwartz

# 10

# THE SUBTLE SELL

If someone asked you to write and deliver a toast, your next question would probably be, "OK, but for what kind of event?" A wedding? An anniversary? A birthday? A retirement party? While your toast might have similar themes for all of those events, each situation would require a different spin on those themes.

The same is true when you're asked to speak about your business. While some core aspects of your presentation may stay the same, your speech will change depending on what is appropriate for a particular situation. This is why it's never a good idea to practice one version of a presentation and refuse to ever change it. You may find yourself being asked to speak about your business in a variety of different situations: networking groups, investor meetings, trade conferences, education events, college groups, sales presentations, etc. Here are a few factors to consider when deciding how to craft a presentation:

**1. How many people will be in the audience?**

An intimate setting will allow for a more interactive

presentation, while a larger group will need more of a lecture style presentation.

## 2. How well do I know the group?

If you're a member of this group and they already know what you do, you'll need to spend less time explaining your background.

## 3. Is this audience a target market for me?

If you'll be speaking to people who need your product or service, you'll be trying to sell. If not, you'll be asking for referrals.

## 4. Is a hard sell appropriate?

This last question can be the toughest to answer so we'll explore it in more detail.

### Hard Sell or a Subtle Sell?

When you're giving a sales presentation, free marketing event, or networking talk, the audience expects to hear a direct sales pitch or a "hard sell." However, you may be asked to speak at a venue where a "hard sell pitch" is not appropriate, or not allowed. Trade conference education sessions, events involving non-profits, or events at educational institutions sometimes fall into this category. You may be tempted to turn down events like this at which you're told not to sell. Don't worry, you can *definitely* still sell your product or service, you just have to change your approach.

In a subtle sell, people still receive information about your product, they still understand how you're different and better than your competition, and they still know where to go to purchase your product, you just haven't directly told them, "Hey, go buy my stuff right now!"

Even in situations where a hard sell *is* appropriate, sprinkling in soft sell techniques throughout your talk can help boost your sales at the end. Here are a few subtle sell strategies to try:

**Product Placement**

Mentioning your product while talking about something else helps people know it exists. For example, let's say you're an organization expert giving an education session at an HR conference about how to manage clutter in the office. You've been told that you can't directly sell your services to the audience, but you know if you could just get them to buy your book, you could convert at least one or two of those sales into clients. Since the session organizers won't let you sell your book at the back of the room, you'll need another way to let them know it exists. That's why you need to work it into the presentation a few times.

As you're talking about one of your key concepts, say something like, "This concept is one of the most misunderstood issues I encounter. It's why I devoted a whole chapter in my book to setting the record straight!" or "I talk much more about this in my book, but here is the nutshell version." In addition, be sure to include that you're an author on your handout. For example, your title could be "10 Organizational Tips You Haven't Tried" presented by Sandra Bailey, author of *The Best Darn Organization Book You'll Ever Read.*

**Name Dropping**

Work testimonials into educational topics. For example, if you're a marketing consultant talking about direct mail postcard designs saying something like, *"I was just able to help someone with this problem last week and he said my few simple design tweaks drastically increased his response rate. Never underestimate the power of good design."*

Or,

*"Someone asked me a great question about this when I was speaking at a conference in Tampa last week."*

Think about what those two statements convey: 1. You're really good at helping people and increasing their sales and 2. You're an in-demand speaker who travels the country, and works with clients nation wide.

## Raffle

Your host might have said you can't sell, but they never said anything about giving things away! Raffles are a great way to sell without selling. At the beginning of the presentation, ask that everyone take a notecard on their way in. Tell them to use the notecard to record any questions they might have during the session and then to keep it handy because it'll be the key to winning some free things at the end. Then, at the end of the talk, instruct everyone to make sure they have at least one question written on the notecard along with their first and last name.

As they are doing this, describe the prize you'll be giving away. This can be a copy of your book, a free consultation, a small sample of your product, or anything else that seems valuable but doesn't actually cost you too much. This is your chance to describe your product in great detail and say how great it is. It's not selling because you're not asking for money. Instead, you're describing the fabulous prize the audience can win that you have generously donated.

After you collect the notecards, have somebody draw one out of the pile, give away the prize, and then also answer the question on the card. Close by saying something like, "if you're one of those people who never wins anything in raffles, like I am, I invite you to come up afterwards and get your question answered. I'm going to be hanging out for a little bit and would love to talk to you."

Let's examine the benefits of the raffle approach:

### 1. It generates engagement

By asking the audience to think of questions, you've given them something to listen for during the presentation. That keeps them engaged.

### 2. It encourages people to talk to you

Once they have their question, they want it answered! Since you can only answer one, they'll have to come talk to you or contact you through your website. Both methods allow you to start a relationship with them.

### 3. You're able to describe your product without selling it

As you're describing the prize the audience is about to win, you're definitely pitching your product, but it doesn't come across as a sales pitch because you're not asking for money.

### 4. You can use it to collect testimonials

Instead of asking for questions, ask people to write down their favorite part of the presentation, or one thing they learned during your speech. Ask them to check a little box on the bottom that says it's OK to use their statement on your website, and you've now just gathered a ton of testimonials to use in future marketing efforts.

### 5. It encourages sales

People love to win things. As you are describing your product, everyone in the audience is picturing themselves winning it. Once they've already pictured themselves with your product, they are more likely to buy it.

## Blog Sign Up

Another way to maximize the soft sell is to "sell" something other than your product. Pass around a clipboard and ask people to sign up for your blog with their email. Ask for as little information as possible because the more you ask, the more it seems like you're selling. If you don't have a blog, you can send out an article you've written recently, or a how-to video the audience will find helpful. Instead of directly selling, you're setting up another touch point for your audience to hear from you. When you send out the email, you'll of course have a link to your website so recipients can learn more. Remember, you want to make it as easy as possible for people to learn more about you and see what you have to offer.

## Get Them To Listen

The most important thing to remember during a subtle sell is that since you're not asking for money on the spot, you have to be memorable enough that people will still remember you either when they get home, or months later when they find themselves in need of your product or service. Refer back to some of the engagement strategies we talked about earlier in the book that help your message stay top of mind.

### 1. Connect to an emotion

People will forget what you tell them, but remember the way you made them feel. Use emotion in your speech. Either make them laugh or make them cry!

### 2. Use stories

Stories are easy to remember and people listen closely because they're curious about the ending. Never pass up an opportunity to use stories to convey your message.

### 3. *Be loud and confident*

When you present, you can't use your talking voice; you have to use your presenting voice. Be louder than you think you need to and project confidence and energy. It makes people perk up and pay attention.

### 4. *Smile*

Smiling is the easiest way to convey emotion, confidence, and friendliness. When people leave your session, they should feel like they know you and can trust you.

### Summary

Don't say no to a speaking opportunity just because you've been told you can't sell. Instead, master the techniques of the "subtle sell" so the audience will still walk away wanting to hire you.

1. Mention your product. Make sure everyone in the audience leaves knowing what it is you sell!

2. Raffle off an item. Raffles are a great way to build excitement about your product without pitching it.

3. Get them to listen. Use engagement strategies to draw the audience in and stay memorable even after the speech is over.

Mastering the subtle sell takes practice and confidence, but once you do, you'll be able to speak anywhere.

Emily Schwartz

# 11

## HANDLE THE UNEXPECTED WITH GRACE

I was in Nashville for the first time speaking at a conference. (By the way, I would not recommend conference travel as a way to see the world, unless you enjoy taking pictures of the inside of hotel ballrooms.) I was pretty excited because the opening Friday night event was a concert at the Grand Ole Opry, and I was pretty sure it'd be the most "touristy" thing I'd get to do all weekend. I plopped down in the first row, exhausted from racing through the airport a few hours earlier to make my connecting flight, and prepared to enjoy some country music.

The concert was great! It was mostly local acts from around the city that whipped the audience up into a frenzy, but as is typical for a speaker at a concert, I couldn't help but be more focused on how the emcee was performing than the musicians. The emcee was a confident young man with a British accent and the kind of easy-going sense of humor that makes you feel as though you've been friends with him since childhood. In other words, the perfect kind of personality to be an emcee.

Right before the last act, the emcee came back on to tell a

few jokes and introduce the headliner. As he finished up his shtick and prepared for the introduction, I watched him stop momentarily. His eyes shifted, and I knew immediately what had happened. The teleprompter was frozen. He wasn't a country music aficionado and couldn't remember the name of the headliner. He was all alone on stage with nobody to feed him a line.

*"Hm,"* I thought to myself. *"How in the world is he going to get out of this one?"*

Without missing a beat, he said, "And now, ladies and gentleman, the moment you've all been waiting for. The man who needs no introduction, please say it with me...."

And at that moment he motioned to the audience who all shouted the name of the singer in unison (which I will omit here so as to save any embarrassment!)

By the irked look on the singer's face, I could tell he knew what had happened, but the audience didn't seem fazed and that's all that mattered. I found the emcee afterwards and congratulated him on a slick and impressive recovery. He chuckled and said,

*"Yeah, it's amazing how prepared we have to be to make this job look easy."*

## The Unexpected

One of the toughest parts of speaking in front of people is to make the whole thing look easy and comfortable, even when things go wrong. As a speaker, you want to appear calm and in charge, as though every minute of the presentation was entirely planned and within your control. Maintaining this appearance is an important part of coming across as an expert to your audience. Remember, you're asking for their business. People give their business to people they trust and who seem like they know what they're doing!

Unfortunately, worrying about the unexpected is one of the biggest reasons people fear public speaking in the first place. *"What if I forget what to say?" "What if the projector breaks?" "What if I get a question I can't answer?" "What if nobody laughs at my jokes?"* Luckily, you can alleviate many of these worries by simply taking the time to prepare.

Think about unexpected problems as existing on a continuum. On the left side of the continuum are things that are very predictable and happen with some degree of frequency. These could be things like, "The projector wasn't working" or "I got a question I couldn't answer." Then, as we move to the right of the continuum, we encounter things that happen less and less frequently. In the middle of the continuum we might have things like "there was a fire drill while I was speaking" or "the meeting was cut short and I didn't have time to give my whole talk."

The right side of the continuum is where it gets fun. This is where you encounter random things you could never predict or prepare for, but have to roll with anyway. The right side is where we find things like, "I got food poisoning and threw up in the middle of my talk," or "the next speaker is running late, so you'll need to fill an extra hour of time." (Both of these things have happened to me.)

**Planning for Technology Failure**

Technology failure is one of the easiest things to prepare for because it happens to everybody. When it comes to computers, projectors, clickers, and sound systems, something is bound to go wrong. When relying on technology, remember these three things:

## 1. Get there early

When you need to hook up a projector or use a sound system, it's always a good idea to arrive early to test all the connections ahead of time. Not only will this put your own mind at ease, but your host will appreciate it too. If something isn't working, you'll have plenty of time to swap in a replacement or figure out a different solution. Remember that setting up technology will always take longer than you think it will and having a few minutes of extra time to sit around is a small price to pay for being prepared.

## 2. Bring extras

Even if your host insists they'll have everything you need, have extras on hand. I always bring my laptop, extension cord, VGA cable, clicker, batteries, and charger to every presentation that requires technology, even if my host insists that all I'll need is a flash drive. Sometimes I'll even have an extra projector in my car (but those are expensive, so don't feel the need to run out and buy one unless you're doing presentations all the time.)

## 3. Be prepared to unplug

If the technology is simply not working and it's visibly stressing your host, be prepared to speak without it. Remember, your PowerPoint is not your speech, it's meant to *supplement* your presentation. You're the speaker and you should be able to deliver your content and make your pitch without the use of visual aids. Practice this in advance so you're prepared. You don't want your audience waiting for your talk to start while you and the host frantically try to work a technology miracle. That doesn't portray confidence.

**Handling Interruptions**

Another problem you might encounter during a presentation is interruptions. This could be a florescent light buzzing, microphone feedback, someone speaking out from the audience, or any number of other things. While you might not be able to predict exactly *what* these interruptions will be, it's important to be prepared to handle them so you maintain your appearance as the "calm, in charge expert" instead of appearing flustered.

*1. Make a joke*

Ignoring an obvious interruption can make everyone a little uncomfortable. It's an "elephant in the room" situation that ends up being even *more* distracting as everyone in the room wonders when you're going to address it. Rather than freak out about the interruption, calmly make a joke about it. I was delivering a sales pitch at a school one summer when the fire alarm starting going off…and kept going off every 15 minutes because they system was being tested. It was extremely distracting and the audience didn't know what to do. After the second time it happened, I stopped the presentation and said, *"Well, I don't know about you, but I feel really safe right now! I'm so glad we all get to experience this chaos together!"* Everybody chuckled and we went on with the presentation.

*2. Address it afterward*

If somebody won't stop calling out and asking questions, acknowledge their requests and say, "I want to have time to address your question thoroughly, so please come up and see my afterwards. We'll have a long chat." Then, refrain from making eye contact with this person as eye contact invites responses.

### 3. Minimize it

A little forethought can go a long way to avoid interruptions in the first place. For example, ask your host to have people silence their cell phones. If you're presenting at a restaurant (a popular place for networking presentations), wait until everyone has paid their checks before beginning so you're not interrupted by wait staff collecting people's money.

### 4. Move past it

Once you've addressed the interruption, resist the temptation to keep bringing it up. At this point, you're probably noticing it more than everyone else and by continuing to reference it, you're not only interrupting your train of thought, but also causing an even bigger distraction. Just talk louder, stand up taller, and move on from the interruption so the audience can move on too and forget about it.

**Forgetting What To Say**

One of the biggest fears in public speaking is forgetting what to say. Not to worry. First of all, if you've prepared and practiced, this is extremely unlikely to happen. Secondly, if it *does* happen, nobody in the audience has your script! Nobody knows that you're going "out of order," skipped a word, or said the wrong thing.

Just keep talking! Speaking is not about memorizing a script it's about conveying stories and ideas. If you're stumbling over a word, just don't say it. Or start talking about something you *do* remember, and come back to your original thought later.

Refrain from saying things like, "Oh goodness, I forgot what I was going to say," or "Wait, no, that's not what I wanted to say next." The audience only knows what you tell them and if you don't tell them you've just messed up, they will never notice.

**Running Out Of Time**

Sometimes the amount of time you were *told* you'd have and the amount of time you *actually* have don't line up. This could be due to a meeting running long, a speaker running over, starting late, or poor planning. The bottom line is, if you arrive at the presentation and find you have less time than you originally thought, don't panic.

When we're crunched for time, our instinct is to cover the same amount of material and just talk faster. Don't fall into that trap! When you talk too fast, your entire message will be lost because people won't be able to keep up. Instead of covering everything, you'll end up covering nothing. Instead, distill your presentation down to your most essential points. Cut out a lengthy introduction, skip your least favorite story or testimonial, skip right to your most essential selling point.

Whatever you do, remain calm and don't appear flustered or rushed. You might be tempted to tell the audience that you were promised more time but you'll have to cut it short. Resist the urge to do that! It makes your host look bad and makes you look unorganized. Roll with the situation and make it look like that's the way you planned it all along.

**If You Absolutely Have To Stop**

By now, you should be a pro at rolling with whatever crazy situation a presentation might throw at you. However, on an extremely rare occasion, you may find yourself unable to continue for one reason or another. Maybe you panicked and need to go regain your composure. Maybe an audience member disrupted your focus and you can't get back on track. If you absolutely need to stop in a presentation, do it gracefully.

## *An Unexpected Stop!*

A few years ago, I woke up with a stomachache the morning of a presentation, but convinced myself I was fine. About 15 minutes into my talk, I realized I was definitely *not* fine and probably had some sort of stomach bug. I realized I had two options: 1. Excuse myself or 2. Push through to the finish and throw up on everyone in the first row. While option number 1 would certainly be embarrassing, option 2 wasn't sounding much better.

After I finished a thought, I said, *"I'm sorry, I need to excuse myself for one moment. I'll be right back."* On the way out of the room I whispered to the host that I was afraid I was about to be sick and that I'd be right back. I barely made it to the bathroom in time before getting a stunning visual reminder of all the foods I'd eaten recently. A few minutes later, after I was sure I'd be able to continue, I walked back into the room standing tall and smiling and greeted the host who was giving some announcements in my absence.

It was clear from the look on everyone's faces that the host had let them know what was going on. I knew I needed to address it, so I quickly made a joke. *"Gosh, I wish I could tell you I was pregnant or some other exciting reason I just got sick in the middle of a presentation. But that's what keeps life interesting right? Let's continue..."*

That was the end of it. The rest of the presentation went fine, and I ended up selling more books than I usually do, presumably because people felt sorry for me! The point of that story is not to scare you, but to show you that you can recover from even the worst circumstances and still turn a presentation into something great.

**Summary**

We can't plan for everything, but we *can* do our best to prevent problems before they occur.

1. Plan for technology to go wrong and bring back-ups with you

2. Move past interruptions quickly and don't let them disrupt your focus

3. Remain calm and roll with whatever is thrown at you. If you stay calm, so will your audience!

The more you speak, the more you'll be prepared for unexpected situations and will still be able to turn a potentially disastrous presentation into a great networking and sales opportunity.

Emily Schwartz

# 12

# ANATOMY OF A PRESENTATION

In the previous chapters, we've dissected the nuts and bolts about how to deliver a great presentation that not only grabs people's attention, but also motivates them to open their wallets. Now it's time to put all the pieces together. Let's use what we've learned to craft a sample 30-minute presentation. Since networking groups are an easy audience to get, and a common sales scenario, we'll start there.

### *Anatomy of a Great Presentation*

(30-minute Networking Presentation)

**The Hook** - (2 minutes) This is where you explain how you make the audiences' lives better. You describe a problem they have and how you solve it with your product or service. Audience engagement is key here. Perhaps you ask them a question, tell them a story, or ask them to respond to a scenario. It's important to play to an *emotion* during the hook. How do you want your audience to *feel*?

**The Background** – (3 minutes) This is where you tell about yourself and your company, without making it sound like you're reading from a resume. Perhaps you say why you love what you do, why you got into the business in the first place

**The Information (Part 1)** – (8 minutes) Give your audience some information about your industry. For example, when I talk about my time management book, this section is usually something like "Three common Time Killers and how to avoid them."

**Story #1 (Testimonial)** – (4 minutes) Tell a story that relates to the information you just gave. This can be in the form of a testimonial, a past client success, or personal experience.

**Information (Part 2)** – (5 minutes) Finish up with a little bit more information. This should be your most important point and one that speaks directly to the audience's need for your product or service.

**The Pitch** - (3 minutes) Since this is a networking presentation, a hard sell is appropriate. What action do you want your audience to take *today* that will help put money in your pocket? Remember, discounts, specials, and raffles encourage people to buy now instead of waiting until later.

**Story #2** - (3 minutes) This should be your "inspirational story," something the audience will remember. It contains a message or moral that sums up your business philosophy or the benefit your product offers to consumers. It finishes with a conclusive ending that cues the audience your presentation is over and it's time to clap.

**Wrap up-** (2 minutes) After your presentation has finished, briefly remind the audience of your pitch and thank them for listening. This is where you can include time for questions if you want to, but remember, it's not a necessity.

Voila! Now you have the structure of a 30-minute networking presentation designed to keep people listening all the way until the end. Not only will they be more likely to buy your service when you're done, but you'll come across as a poised, professional speaker- the kind of person people revere as an expert in the field. Even if they don't buy from you immediately, they'll be more likely to remember you and tell their friends about you.

**Creating Your Own Presentation**

Use the above outline as a guide to create your own presentation. Remember, it's important to assess whether a hard or soft sell is appropriate before you begin writing. Misinterpreting the situation can lead to an awkward presentation. You might need to make it longer or shorter, depending on circumstance, Once your presentation is finished, recognize that it is a constant work-in-progress and isn't set in stone. You'll want to revise it when you see how the audience reacts. Every time you speak, you'll make it better.

**Practice**

"Winging it" is the enemy of a great presentation. No matter how informal you think your talk may be, if you want to come off sounding like a professional, you'll need to practice. Practicing in front of live people is important because you'll be able to gauge reaction. Recruit your family or friends to listen to your talk and try to keep it as "real" as possible. You might even want to videotape yourself the first few times to catch any bad habits you may have that you don't realize.

If stage fright or speaking anxiety is even the slightest issue for you, practice will definitely help. Preparation is the best defense against anxiety.

**Speak First, Sell Second**

Remember, before you can speak so people will buy, you have to first speak so people will *listen*. If your speeches aren't generating the sales you want, your prices might be too high, your target audience might be wrong, you might not be doing enough to differentiate yourself from your competition...or all of that stuff could be *perfect* and you're simply not speaking in a way that conveys it. Before you tweak your sell, tweak your presentation. You may not think of yourself as a professional speaker, but if part of your job is networking or selling, then that's exactly what you are. It's time you start treating yourself that way.

Good luck on your speaking journey. Now go and earn that standing ovation!

How to Speak so People Will Buy

Emily Schwartz

# ABOUT THE AUTHOR

Dr. Emily Schwartz is an international speaker on the subjects of time management, education, and communication. As a public speaking coach, she has helped hundreds of people improve their skills and polish their message including students, salespeople, receptionists, business owners, and more. With a strong background in education, she holds a Ph.D. and Master's degree from Arizona State University and a Bachelor's degree from The University of Southern California. She currently lives in Phoenix with her husband, daughter, and two dogs.

Check out Emily's time management page at

## www.TheTimeDiet.org

For coaching inquires, please email:

## Emily@TheTimeDiet.org

**Other Books by Emily Schwartz**

The Time Diet: Digestible Time Management
The Time Diet: Time Management for College Survival
Life in Cut Time: Time Management for Music Teachers

Available in paperwork or e-book format on Amazon.com

www.ingramcontent.com/pod-product-compliance
Lightning Source LLC
LaVergne TN
LVHW021352080426
835508LV00020B/2246